The Abel & Cole Veg Box Companion

by Keith Abel

A complete guide to enjoying
all the veg life throws at you

Contents

Introduction

I get phone calls all the time from my friend Suzie saying, 'Keith, what on earth am I supposed to do with this weird vegetable you've sent me?!?'

People get into the routine of peas and potatoes but explode with excitement when they work out what to do with a new vegetable. It's a bit like a physicist discovering a new bit of the Higgs boson.

After two decades of veg box evangelism, my favourite customer feedback isn't 'getting a veg box from you is like Christmas every week', or even 'we're eating much more healthily since getting a veg box from you'.

It's the floods of emails and letters that say 'I never thought I'd say this, but thank you so much for introducing me to celeriac (fennel, curly kale, kohlrabi...) I would never have tried it, and I love it!'

That's what eating seasonally with a veg box is all about. It's being adventurous in a 'it doesn't matter if it all goes wrong' kind of way and discovering loads of new food that you really love.

Be bold. Break away from broccoli. Sauté that salsify with self assurance.

And here's the secret: keep it simple. You don't need a list of ingredients as long as a leek. You just need a leek.

With a couple of spices from the cupboard, a bit of olive oil or butter and maybe a lemon, I absolutely guarantee you can whip up something that tastes fantastic. Take that, Saturday Kitchen!

This book is to stop cooking feeling like a chore. The seven dwarves hit the nail on the head with all that whistling. (If only that apple was organic.) Personally I prefer dancing… badly.

So, pour yourself a nice glass of wine and get your favourite partner/playlist/pooch to keep you company. Switch off your phone, turn up the stereo and in the same time it takes to microwave a ready meal, you'll have made something healthy and delicious, and you'll feel like you've got a Large Hadron Collider in your kitchen.

So here you go Suzie, you'll have to think of another reason to phone me up now.

Keith Abel

So farm, so good

In the beginning there were potatoes.

I was on holiday with my gorgeous new girlfriend, Chippy, in the summer of 1988 when I found out I hadn't done quite as well as I'd hoped in my bar exams.

The thought of leaving sunny Spain to go back to grey London and cram for re-sits didn't appeal. So I stayed in the sunshine for another few weeks (to make sure Chippy fell totally in love with me, which she did, and we're still besotted. Well most of the time... come on it's been 24 years).

When I got back to London reality kicked in. But I had a plan.

I convinced my mum and my two friends Paul Cole and Jules Allen to get up very, very, very early one morning and come with me to New Covent Garden Market. Before long we were in possession of a ginormous load of potatoes, divvying them into 10lb bags.

The question remained, would the kind people of Catford buy spuds from a posh git with a suntan, still dragging his mother around with him?

They did.

We had such a laugh meeting them all.

Now, at this time, I have to admit that I didn't know much about organic vegetables. Everything that grew was organic, surely?

Then I met a chap called Bernard* who told me to ask what was sprayed on my potatoes.

When a farmer showed me a shed full (literally) of chemicals with skull & crossbone symbols all over them, it just didn't feel right.

Before long the only spuds we delivered were from an organic, agro-chemical-free farm and my loyal customers started wondering if they might have a more varied diet. The Essential Organic Veg Box was born.

There were a few false starts, mostly because we hadn't quite twigged that if you decide to set up anything that involves food in a really hot Summer, you kind of need a fridge.

*We still get organic veg from Bernard's farm in Devon, although his paragliding son Dave now runs the show.

We've got some really good fridges now, even on the back of our vans and we deliver ethically sourced veg, milk, eggs, meat, fish and all sorts to happy homes all over the country.

And our principles are still the same. We speak to our farmers every day, we know how to have a giggle, and we're still enormously grateful to our customers for keeping the whole venture alive.

Me, just after I heard my exam results

A little housekeeping

Hands up who likes breaking rules? Me too. I give you full permission to bend almost all of the recipes in this book (follow the baking rules though, otherwise you'll get flat cakes).

Use what you've got to hand. Plum out of spinach? Use a cabbage. Need a leek? Use an onion. Need an onion? Use a leek. Or a shallot.

Use dried herbs instead of fresh and if you don't have any herbs at all – no worries. Your veg will still rock.

Who are you calling a mug?

Like my teenage son Hugo, our recipes are pretty laid back, so you can use as little or as much of most ingredients as you like. A mug and a handful generally mean; whatever you fancy.

Capital V for Parmesan

Traditionally, Parmesan is not suitable for vegetarians, but there's plenty of vegetarian stuff around these days. In most recipes you can replace it for cheddar or another cheese, or skip it entirely.

Autumn

Leaves, leaves, leaves, bonfires, pumpkins,
chunky knit cardigans, chutney making

Stuffed Squash

Autumn

Autumn starts with the Autumn Equinox on 22nd or 22rd September. Autumn ends on 20th December with the Winter Solstice.

Look out for

Apples in September

Conkers in October

Squash in November

Kohlrabi in December

Things to do in Autumn

Make chutney (homemade Christmas presents)

Take up knitting, and never buy a scarf again

Make sloe gin

Get back into porridge (not literally)

Re-discover Monopoly

Eat as many varieties of apples and squash as you can

In a right pickle

Got more tomatoes, apples or beetroot than you can shake a black salsify at? Make chutney. All you need is vinegar, sugar and fruit or veg, and your favourite chutney recipe.

If you're reusing old glass jars, clean them (plus lids) in really hot soapy water, or put in the dishwasher on the hottest setting. Dry on a clean tea towel or kitchen paper.

When your chutney's nearly ready, put the jars and lids in a cold oven. Heat to 150°C/Gas 2 for 15 mins. Take the jars hot from the oven (use gloves!). Spoon in the just-cooked chutney. Seal immediately.

Because vinegar causes some lids to rust, you need to make sure metal lids don't come into contact with chutney. Kilner jars are ideal, but most jam jar lids have a plastic-like covering on the inside.

Autumn is... apples

Britain's good for lots of things, but it's not exactly exotic. Pineapples might be exciting, but did you know that there are over 2,000 varieties of apples we could grow here?

Since the 1950s, over half our English orchards have been abandoned, as cheap imports filled our shops and British farmers couldn't compete on price.

We champion farmers who stand by their traditional fruit and veg. Having more than 15 varieties of apple in our boxes during the UK apple season is an utter delight and more exciting than a hundred guavas could ever hope to be.

Fennel

Fennel has a long and illustrious history. Revered by Hippocrates, Heston Blumenthal, and a thirteenth century physician who said, "He who sees fennel and gathers it not, is not a man but a devil." That's possibly taking things a little far, but it is handy to have in the fridge.

Fennel fashions

Whisper

Shave off wispy slivers with a veg peeler. Super with orange segments, fresh mint and goat's cheese. Or in pasta with garlic, chilli and Parmesan. Or, add to potato and smoked mackerel salad with a lemony, crème fraîche dressing.

Bubbler

Slice into thin panels. Fry in oil with garlic till tender. Season. Add a splash of cream and stock. Layer in a baking dish with a little cheese and crushed toasted walnuts. Top with breadcrumbs. Grill till bubbly and golden.

Barber

Fennel loves smoke. Cut down from the top into quarters but don't cut all the way through. Sprinkle freshly chopped chilli into the gap and add a little butter. Wrap in foil and pop on the barbecue for 30–40 mins.

Bowler

Take inspiration from Mediterranean fish soups, and simmer diced fennel with lots of tomatoes and saffron. Fennel cubes are also lovely in chicken soup.

Frugal fennel

Save all the trimmings for the stock pot or pop herby fronds in a teacup and add hot water. Good for the digestion, 'pparently.

VEGAN
Sizzled Fennel Steaks

These are so easy, but they look impressive. You could make them the base of a salad with mozzarella, chilli and basil leaves piled on top.

Slice fennel into thick panels. Season and drizzle with oil. Fry on both sides till tender and starting to brown a little (about 10–15 mins). If you have a lemon to hand, squeeze some juice over before serving. Tastes of Italy.

- 1 or 2 fennel bulbs
- Sea salt and freshly ground pepper
- Olive oil

Prep: 5 mins
Cook: 10 mins
Serves: 2

♡ **Fennel loves...**

Orange, olives, goat's cheese, fresh mint, basil, halloumi, mozzarella, Parmesan, fish.

Kohlrabi

Kohlrabi, me ole mucker. Always greeted with 'Whaaaaat is this UFO in my veg box!?' Those in the know love you for your crisp, fresh broccoli-stalk-like-ness. Part of the brassica family, kohlrabi is worth getting to know.

Kohl to action

Kohlrawbi

Kohlrabi is best eaten raw. At Abel & Cole, the more veg-obsessed you are, the better. Eating raw veg in the pub on a Friday is almost a sport. Aubergine is really not good, but kohlrabi is. Just peel, slice and crunch. Or cut into cubes or matchsticks and add to salad.

Grahtini

Not sure how you feel about this alien veg? Gratin is the way forward. Peel and thinly slice along with some spuds, chopped rosemary, cream and garlic. Layer and bake slowly till tender inside and crisp and golden on top.

Krispy

Carve the skin off your kohlrabi and cut into rounds. Halve these and dip into a batter made from half a mug of seasoned self-raising white flour and half a mug of beer or sparkling water. Dip and deep fry till golden. Batter and fry up a few sprigs of parsley too. Lovely with sea salt and lemon juice.

♡ Kohlrabi loves...

Cheddar, bacon, peanut butter, cream, mascarpone, parsley, potatoes, garlic, apple, radish, orange, tangy salad dressings.

VEGAN OR VEGETARIAN OR OMNIVOROUS

Hella's Creamy Kohlrabi Soup

Hella works with our European farmers. She speaks a bazzillion languages and talks faster than an auctioneer after a triple espresso. And she loves kohlrabi.

Gently fry the kohlrabi, onion and garlic in butter or oil over a medium-low heat for a few mins.

Add the spuds and stock and simmer till the veg are soft enough to whizz up. Pop the veg and parsley in the blender. Let it cool a bit first as the pressure from the steam can make the lid blow off (speaking from experience). Purée till smooth.

Transfer it back to the pan to heat up. Taste. Season with salt, pepper and a touch of lemon juice and zest, and perhaps some nutmeg.

Serve with a dollop of crème fraîche, a bit more parsley and even some crispy pancetta or little bits of bacon, if you fancy.

- 1 kohlrabi or 300g broccoli stalks, peeled and diced
- 1 garlic clove, finely chopped
- 1 onion, finely chopped
- A nugget of butter or splash of olive oil
- 1 medium potato, peeled and diced
- 500ml veg or chicken stock
- Sea salt and freshly ground pepper
- A handful of fresh parsley, plus more to serve
- ½ lemon, juice and zest
- A grating of fresh nutmeg and a dollop of crème fraîche (optional)

Prep: 15 mins

Cook: 20 mins

Serves: 2

Romanesco cauliflower

Fractally actually wonderful weird space veg, romanesco cauliflower is the swirliest food in the universe. The florets follow a fractal pattern that makes them more cosmic than a transcendental meditation retreat.

Fractal fixes

Roasted flourish

Roast these fab florets with cumin seeds, paprika and chilli powder. Add some lemon or lime wedges. Serve with lamb chops, Puy lentils and fresh coriander. Or with chorizo, chickpeas and rice.

Inspiral curries

Toss romanesco florets (raw or roasted) into your favourite curry. They soak up flavours like a sponge.

Fractal pasta

Sizzle smallish romanesco florets in a frying pan with olive oil. Season well. Finish with lemon juice and zest. Swirl into pasta with pesto.

♡ **Romanesco loves...**

Paprika, cumin, coriander, lemon, lime, lentils, pesto, Parmesan, lamb, Parma ham wrapped roasted fish.

Abracadabra Romanesco

This magical recipe is so simply delicious that it'll disappear as fast as chocolate cake at a children's birthday party.

Preheat the oven to 200°C/Gas 6. Boil the kettle.

Trim the base of your cauli, so it'll sit flat. Keep some of the green leaves on, they'll go nice and crisp and toasty.

Put your cauli in a big lidded pot and pour in the water you've just boiled, so it comes about half way up. Cover and cook on medium heat till tender (5–10 mins). Drain.

Stand the cauli upright on a roasting tray. Drizzle with olive oil. Season well. Quarter your lemon and put it next to the cauli.

Roast till it picks up a nice bit of colour (about 20 mins but depends on size). Make sure it doesn't touch the top of the oven. Squeeze the roasted lemon over. Finish with grated cheese and/or some spices (smoky paprika, a little chilli or cumin). Cut into wedges and serve.

- 1 whole romanesco or regular cauliflower
- A drizzle of olive oil
- Sea salt and freshly ground pepper
- 1 lemon
- A grating of Parmesan and/or a dusting of spice (optional)

Prep: 5–10 mins, depending on size

Cook: 25 mins

Serves: 2–4

Storage tips

Keep romanesco in the fridge for up to a week. Don't freeze these fractals - they'll go all mushy.

Spinach

Good things come in leafy packages. If you've not had a veg box or an allotment, you'll know spinach as baby leaves that reduce down to practically nothing at the hint of a saucepan. Those baby leaves are gorgeous raw, but main crop spinach is the stuff you want to cook with. It's got bigger leaves, bigger flavour, and is better suited to our organic British fields.

> ♡ **Spinach loves...**
>
> Lemon, cream, bacon, egg, all sorts of cheese, garlic, onion, potatoes, nutmeg.

Greener gastronomy

'Allo Saag

Your curries will love spinach. The flavour mingles marvellously with onions, potatoes and spices like turmeric, cinnamon, ginger, cloves and chilli.

Baby don't leaf me

Baby spinach is lush finely chopped and added to scrambled eggs. Add a handful of grated cheddar and a dash of chilli sauce too. Stuff into a warm pitta for a portable breakfast.

VEGETARIAN
Creamed Spinach with Lemon Breadcrumbs

A lemony twist on a classic. Delicious with pan-fried plaice and a glass of chilled white wine.

Blitz or grate the stale bread into crumbs. Season with lemon zest, sea salt and pepper. Fry in a splash of olive oil till golden and crisp. Set aside.

Melt the butter in a large pan. Pile in the spinach. Season well. Gently stir till it's wilted yet still bright and glossy. Pop into a colander. Gently press out any excess liquid. Return to the pan. Squeeze in some lemon juice. Dust with nutmeg. Taste and adjust seasoning accordingly.

Swirl in the Parmesan and crème fraîche. Warm through briefly. Scatter breadcrumbs over the top and serve.

- 2 stale slices of bread
- 1 lemon, juice and zest
- Sea salt and freshly ground pepper
- A splash of olive oil
- A nugget of butter
- A bag of spinach or chard
- Ground nutmeg
- 100–125g crème fraîche
- A large handful of grated Parmesan

Prep: 5 mins
Cook: 15 mins
Serves: 2–4

Storage tips
Spinach loves the fridge.
The sooner it gets there,
the crisper it'll stay.

Lighten up

How to make your Jack O'Lantern and eat it

You will need

One pumpkin
One grown up
One sharp knife
One seriously spooky design

To make your lantern

Place your pumpkin on a large board.

Cut a wide circle around the stalk, and pull it out - this is your lid.

Scrape out the seeds and stringy bits using a large metal spoon. Save the seeds - they're delicious roasted with a pinch of salt and spice (see overleaf).

Use a knife to loosen the inner flesh of the pumpkin. Scrape a good layer out, use your spoon to help. Don't throw it away though – it'll make a brilliant soup or a cheesy gratin.

Draw your design on the skin with a pen. Carefully cut through the lines (with a small sharp knife) and push out the bits.

Pop a tealight inside the pumpkin, light it up, place the lid on and send us a photo.

And now to make soup

Follow this for squash soup too

Finely chop an onion and a garlic clove. Sizzle in olive oil till glossy and soft. Roughly chop the pumpkin flesh and add to the pan. Season well.

Sizzle till it's pretty much turned to mash. Taste. When it's delicious, it's ready. Add a touch of sugar to bring out the sweetness if needed.

Pour in enough chicken or veg stock to just cover. A dash of sherry is also good. Let it bubble up. Then blitz till smooth. Add a drizzle of cream and some herbs or spice (sage is nice). Yummy with cheesy soldiers.

Watch the video on our Abel & Cole YouTube channel.

Squash

Hokkaido, delicata, acorn, sunshine. Not next season's must have nail varnish colours, but squash. Our fantastic farmers grow some very interesting veg and Jono Smales and Clive Martin harvest a smorgasbord of squashes for our boxes each year.

Cutting & peeling

Carving pumpkins can be fun, but it's a bit tricky. If you're not carving one to make a ghoulish lantern, here's probably the best tip for peeling squash and pumpkins: don't.

The skin is edible and rather tasty, especially on thin-skinned varieties.

Thick skin isn't as tasty, but cook your squash with the skin on and it's much easier to remove afterwards (it'll be softer and you can just pull it away).

When it comes to cutting, the trick is to just use the tip of your knife. Then carefully work your way around the circumference. Once halved, spoon the seeds out (save them for planting, or roasting then eating) then cut into wedges.

Seedy

Remove the pumpkin strands off your seeds and drizzle with oil. Arrange in a single layer on a roasting tray and season. Cook alongside your squash. They'll take 10–15 mins at about 180°C/Gas 4.

Storage tips

Squash will last for ages stored somewhere reasonably cool and dry. I've known squash to sit in a fruit bowl for months and still be in great nick.

♡ **Squash loves...**

Chilli, cinnamon, nutmeg, onion, roast chicken, ginger, grains, roasted garlic.

Bish, bosh, squash

Lazy squashy mash

This is so lazy there's actually no mashing to do. It works best with round varieties like onion, pale blue confection, kabocha or sunshine.

Halve your squash horizontally. Spoon out the seeds. Rub the inside with olive oil. Pop garlic cloves in each half. Season well. Roast at 200°C/Gas 6 till really soft.

Sprinkle over some spice or herbs and a touch more butter or olive oil.

Job done. Just season to taste and scoop the mash straight from the squash.

Sweet things

Squash is technically a fruit. So it's absolutely brilliant in baking, puddings and sweet treats.

Add a handful of raw grated squash to your favourite carrot cake mixture instead of carrots.

Superb squash salad

Try roasted or pan-fried slices with leaves, toasted walnuts, apple slices and a blue cheese dressing.

Or grate it raw, as you would a carrot. Dress with lime juice, fresh ginger, chilli, a splash of soy sauce, sesame oil, toasted seeds and fresh coriander. Gorgeous.

Stuffed Squash with Zingy Tahini Dressing

This zingy number is far from stuffy. Use pretty much any squash you want. We've listed our favourites.

Heat your oven to 200°C/Gas 6.

Halve your squash. Spoon out the seeds. Rub with olive oil, inside and out. Season well.

Roast for 20–35 mins, till tender and just golden. Put quinoa or bulgar wheat into a warm lidded pan. Let it toast for a mo. Add a drop of olive oil and a pinch of salt and pepper. Stir and sizzle for a sec.

Add a mug of water. Let it bubble up. Cover. Reduce the heat and simmer for 10 mins or till all the water is guzzled up. Keep covered for a further 5–10 mins after you've turned the heat off.

Once the grains are nice and fluffy, fold in the chilli, ginger, spring onions, garlic, citrus juice and zest, honey or agave, soy sauce and a splash of olive oil. Mix, taste, adjust seasoning if needed. Then fold in the herbs.

Let the squash cool a little once cooked. Spoon the stuffing into the ready made vegetabowls.

For the dressing: put the tahini in a bowl. Squeeze in the orange juice. Stir till smooth. Add a little more tahini or juice till it's dressing consistency. Add soy sauce to taste, and a little chilli if you like. Finish with finely chopped parsley and a drizzle or dollop of dressing over the stuffed squash.

This is fab at any temperature and is lovely with salad.

- 1 harlequin squash, 2 gem squash or a butternut squash
- Olive oil
- Sea salt and freshly ground pepper
- ½ mug of quinoa or bulgar wheat
- 1 mug of water
- ½ red chilli, finely chopped
- 3–4 cm piece of fresh ginger, finely grated
- 3–4 spring onions, thinly sliced
- 1 garlic clove, finely chopped
- 2–3 tbsp fresh orange and/or lime juice, plus zest
- 1 tsp honey or agave syrup
- A dash of soy sauce
- A handful of fresh mint, coriander and/or parsley, roughly chopped

For the tahini dressing:
- 2 tbsp tahini
- 1 orange, juice
- A drop of soy sauce
- A bit of freshly chopped red chilli (optional)
- A good pinch of finely chopped parsley

Prep: 10 mins

Cook: 35 mins

Serves: 2–4

Sweet potato

As much as I adore regular white tubers, sweet potatoes are a healthier shade of spud. They're lower on the glycemic index and are full of vitamin A.

Sweet inspiration

Couch potato

The easiest way to prepare sweet potatoes is to do... not much.

Roast your sweet potato whole for about an hour and you'll have the most deliciously sweet jacket spud ever.

Slice it open and pile in some grated cheddar or a dollop of crème fraîche.

Vegan? A drizzle of sesame oil, lime juice, ginger, chilli and fresh coriander is good.

Use sweet potatoes in our potato bread recipe on page 224. Add a little chilli to spice it up.

> ♡ **Sweet potatoes love...**
>
> Chives, rosemary, red lentils, sausages, soy sauce, ginger, spring onions, chilli, paprika, satay sauce.

Mash in a flash (in a pan)

Sweet potatoes cook quite quickly. For mash in a flash, peel your sweet potato and cut into small cubes.

Place a frying pan over medium heat. Add a splash of olive oil. Pop the spuds into the pan. Stir so they're coated in oil. Cover and cook for 10–15 mins. Check a few times. When they're soft, mash with a bit of butter and season. Cosy.

> **Storage tips**
>
> Keep your sweet potatoes in a paper bag in a cool, dry place.
>
> If you want to freeze them, peel and grate first. Pop into a plastic container. Use the grated sweet potato (frozen or defrosted) instead of carrots in carrot cake.
>
> Chunks of sweet potato, like cubes or chip-shapes, need to be roasted or lightly boiled before freezing.

Sweet Potato Chips
with Spiced Crème Fraîche

Mix the crème fraîche or yogurt with a good pinch of salt, a grating of lime zest and a good squeeze of juice, cumin, chilli powder and coriander or parsley.

Taste. Adjust seasoning, if needed. You may want more lime juice or chilli powder. Give it a decent kick as it contrasts beautifully with the sweet potatoes. When you're happy with it, pop in the fridge to chill.

Place a large frying pan over high heat. Add a 1 cm deep pool of sunflower oil. Once hot, add the sweet potatoes and a pinch of salt and pepper. Lower the heat to medium.

Cook till golden on all sides. Check and turn them frequently.

Add a squeeze of lime juice, a good pinch of paprika and salt to your chips. Serve hot with the cold dip.

- 2–3 sweet potatoes, peeled and chipped
- 150g crème fraîche, or natural or Greek yogurt
- Sea salt and freshly ground pepper
- 1 lime, juice and zest
- ¼ tsp ground cumin
- A good pinch (nearly a tsp) of chilli powder
- 1 tbsp finely chopped fresh coriander or parsley
- A good splash of sunflower oil
- A pinch of paprika

Prep: 10 mins

Cook: 20 mins

Serves: 2–4

Turnip

Whilst Baldrick may like turnips every day, they don't turn up in our boxes very often. When they do, rather than making you feel like Baldrick, or an extra from Cadfael, they're a bit of a treat.

Abel & Cole customer tips

Casie's casserole

Diced turnip, chopped onions, rosemary, beef and beer make a wicked stew. Fry the veg. Brown the beef. Add the herbs. Cover with beer and stock and let it gently bubble for a few hours. Dreamy with dumplings.

Trudy's turnips

Raw turnips can vary from mild to very peppery, like radishes. Matchstick or grate and add to coleslaws, sprinkle over salad, or use in place of celeriac in remoulade.

Ruth's turnoverips

Turnip and bacon, uh-huh. Fry up chopped leek or onion, and bacon. Add grated turnip and heat through. Dollop a spoonful in the middle of 5 cm puff pastry circles. Seal the edges with a fork. Cook in a 200°C/Gas 6 oven till golden.

♡ **Turnip loves...**

Lemon, paprika, sea salt, black pepper, bacon, cream, garlic, thyme, crème fraîche, apple, cabbage, roast chicken.

Storage tips

Turnips are ok at cool room temperature. However they'll keep longer in the fridge.

Smokin' Turnip Layers

If you want to skip the bacon, smoked sea salt will do very nicely instead.

Preheat the oven to 180°C/Gas 4. Peel the turnips and slice into thin discs. Cut large turnip discs into halves or quarters.

Crisp up the bacon in a smallish pan. As it cooks, mix the sliced turnips in a bowl with garlic, olive oil, salt, pepper and thyme. Add to the pan. Sizzle for a min. Add the wine or cider. Let it bubble up, soften the veg and let the liquid reduce down a bit (15–20 mins). Swirl in the crème fraîche. Scatter more thyme and pepper on top.

If your pan's not ovenproof, tumble everything into a baking dish. Pop in the oven till brown (about 30 mins). Delicious with a crisp green salad and roast chicken.

- 2 large or 4 small turnips
- 4 rashers of smoky bacon, cut into lardons
- 2 garlic cloves, minced
- A few glugs of olive oil
- Sea salt and freshly ground pepper
- A few sprigs of fresh thyme, leaves only
- A glass of white wine or cider
- 200g crème fraîche or cream

Prep: 15 mins

Cook: 45 mins

Serves: 4

SMASHING and NICELY

Do the mashed potato. Or the mashed celeriac, the mashed swede, the mashed parsnip, the mashed carrot, the mashed squash...

MASH UP

ROAST FIRST, MASH LATER

Roasting (vs boiling) gives veg a richer, more intense flavour. It works with this bunch.

The no peel potato mash

For the best mashed potatoes ever, bake your spuds like you're making a jacket potato.

Once they're done and have cooled a tiny bit, halve, scoop out the flesh then mash with a little butter or olive oil.

Squash, any squash

Halve if it's a big one (it'll reduce cooking time). Small squash can be shoved in the oven whole, then cut in half once cooked. Once roasted, remove the seeds and scoop out the flesh.

Mash with a little butter, milk, olive oil or cream. (Try a dollop of mascarpone, it's gorgeous.)

Swede, celeriac, parsnips, kohlrabi, Jerusalem artichokes and carrots

Peel 'em. Cut 'em. Toss with oil and sea salt. Lay on a pre-heated roasting tray. Roast till soft. Mash with a fork or masher, or blitz in a food processor with the seasoning of your choice.

MASH UP, SPLASH OUT

Mash is far more than a modest accompaniment. Take it from the boring to the bombastic and splash out by adding some attention grabbing flavours to it.

Hot mash

Freshly grated horseradish (or a dollop from a jar), black pepper, lemon zest and/or finely chopped sorrel leaves.

Monster mash

Chuck some kale, cavolo nero, rocket, watercress or any other strong-flavoured green leaves into a food processor. Blitz for a sec to chop the leaves into a near-pesto state. Fold through your mash. Finish with a dollop of mustard and a knob of salted butter.

Asian mash

Liven your mash up with a bit of coconut milk, finely chopped chilli and grated ginger. Finish with a dash of soy sauce and little bits of chopped coriander leaves. Lovely in carrot mash.

Apples

Cast your mind back to the 1400s (you might have to use your imagination). Picture orchards everywhere bearing hundreds of apple varieties. Not an easy image to conjure, seeing that cheap imported fruit has made many of our orchards redundant. Luckily, native varieties are enjoying something of a comeback. Make sure you buy British when you can, and we'll see even more orchards restored.

> ♡ **Apples love...**
> Cheddar, peanut butter, caraway, ginger, nutmeg, cinnamon, cloves, cardamom, walnuts, black pepper and olive oil, pork, tarragon, sage.

There's more than one way to slice an apple

Julienne, Julienne, wherefore art thou Julienne

Julienne is a fancy word for little sticks. Apples cut into little sticks are delicious, especially in salads and coleslaws.

Star crossed lovers

For a beautiful star pattern, formed by the seeds, slice an apple horizontally into discs. Children love them.

Greatest hits

Grated apple is perfect swirled through simmering porridge, a sausage stuffing mix, or a freshly whisked batch of American style pancakes.

Cubism

Throw frozen diced apple into a blender with yogurt, orange juice, nutmeg and honey for a delicious smoothie. Apple cubes are pleasing in salad, for a surprising crunch of sweetness.

Crumbleism

If you want crumble with a really tender, appley saucy base, slice your apples into thin wisps using a veg peeler. This is a great method for apple sauce too. Slowly simmer the wisps in a pan with a drop of water and a speckle of sugar till it melts.

VEGAN OR VEGETARIAN
Baked Bramleys

Bramleys are delicious baked with stuff inside them, although this will work with any apple. I've listed my favourite stuffing mix, but get creative and experiment with what you have.

Preheat oven to 200°C/Gas 6.

Make a shallow cut (no deeper than 1 cm) around the middle (circumference) of each apple – this lets it expand without exploding.

Mix the remaining ingredients. Sit the apples in a roasting dish and pack the mix into the cores of the apples. Be generous.

Bake for about 40 mins, till the apples are tender and plump. Check halfway through cooking as smaller apples will cook a little faster. Serve with yogurt or cream.

- 4 Bramley apples, cored
- 5 dates, stoned and finely chopped
- 15g dark chocolate, finely chopped
- 4 tbsp almonds, toasted and finely chopped
- A pinch of ground cinnamon
- 1 tbsp brandy or orange juice
- Cream or vanilla (or butterscotch) yogurt, to serve (optional)

Prep: 10 mins
Cook: 40 mins
Serves: 4

Any Apple Bread

A sort of cakey, soda-like wholemeal loaf. It's brilliant warm with butter and honey for breakfast, or with cheese and a bowl of soup for lunch.

Preheat the oven to 180°C/Gas 4.

Brush a 1 ltr non-stick loaf tin (approx 20 x 10 cm) with oil or butter. Coat with a dusting of flour – the old fashioned way to prevent it from sticking.

Combine the dry ingredients. Fold in the grated apples (leave the skin on, if organic). Top with the wet ingredients and nuts and/or dried fruit, if using (save some nuts to scatter on top).

Gently fold all the ingredients together (remember to whisk your egg first.) Be careful not to over-mix.

Spoon the mixture into the tin. Dot the reserved nuts over the top.

Bake for 30 mins, or till a knife inserted in the centre comes out clean.

Let it cool for 10–15 mins before removing from the tin and serving.

- A little oil or butter to grease the tin
- 150g plain flour
- 200g wholemeal flour
- ½ tsp salt
- 1 tsp bicarbonate of soda
- 1 large or 2 smaller apples, peeled and coarsely grated
- 50g butter, melted
- 2 tbsp honey
- 1 egg, whisked
- 250ml apple juice
- A few handfuls of chopped nuts and/or dried fruit (optional)

Prep: 10 mins
Cook: 30 mins
Serves: 6–8

Storing tips

Autumn apples are fine at room temperature, although each variety has its particular peccadilloes. By late Winter and early Spring, store English apples in the fridge.

To store home grown apples, wrap each apple in newspaper, arrange them in a single or double layer in a crate and store in a cool, dry place.

The rules of conkers

Remember the days when kids spent all day outside? A piece of paper to play with, if you were lucky. Then a quick telling off before bed (which was 5pm). Happy days.

How to prepare your winning conker

Drill a hole in your conker of choice (grown up only activity).

Thread a 40 cm long piece of string through and tie a knot to keep the conker on the string.

The rules

(As developed over many years in the playgrounds of England.)

There should be 20 cm (8 inches) between knuckle and nut. Be precise. This is a game of skill.

Oldest person goes first. Each player takes three alternate strikes at the opponent's conker.

The striker wraps their conker string round their hand. They then take the conker in the other hand and draw it back for the strike.

Each attempted strike must be clearly aimed at the nut. No deliberate knuckle hits, boys.

The person holding the conker must hold it still.

If the strings tangle, the first player to call 'strings' gets an extra shot.

If a player drops their conker, or it's knocked from their hand, the other player can shout 'stamps' and jump on it.

However, if its owner cries 'no stamps' first, there should be no jumping.

The surviving conker is the winner. A small piece of nut or skin remaining on the string doesn't count, it must be enough to mount an attack.

A nut knocked from the string but not smashed may be rethreaded and the game continued.

Scoring

A victorious conker assumes the score of all its victim's previous foes.

Thus, in a contest between two fresh conkers, the winner would then have a score of 1 (known as a 'one-er'). If it then beat another three 'one-er's, it would become a 'four-er'.

Apple rings

For centuries we've grown apples over the Summer, harvested them in Autumn, and stored them through the Winter.

My favourite way to store apples is to dry them. They're a great snack, pretty on cakes and also, for the crafters out there, a contender for the best natural Christmas decoration.

Dried Apple Rings

Core your apple. Leave the skin on. Thinly slice.

Mix the salt into a bowl of water. Dip the apple rings in the water.

Shake dry. String them up on a stick. Make sure you leave a bit of space between each ring.

Tie the ends of the stick with string. Hang somewhere high and dry. Let the apple rings dry for 4–5 days.

Store in an airtight container. Pretty if put on cakes, sweet loaves or fruit muffins before baking.

• 3–4 apples
• 1 tsp sea salt
• A bowl of cold water
• A clean wooden stick
• Some string

Prep: 15 mins
Drying: 4–5 days
Makes: Enough to fill a jam jar or two

Chiramoya

This highly evolved fruit has sussed out our penchant for creamy fruit desserts, and has got a one-up on food scientists the world over.

Also known as custard apples, these are, as you'd imagine, sweet and sort of custardy.

Abel & Cole-er Sara Haglund, who helped out lots on this book, says: "I eat them when they are super ripe and soft. Just tear them apart, spoon out the flesh and spit out the stones, watermelon seed bullet style."

She's right, please make sure you don't try to eat the seeds - they'll win, your teeth will lose.

Storing tips

Allow these dudes to ripen at room temp. A ripe chiramoya should yield to gentle pressure and will have browner skin.

Once ripe, chiramoya can be refrigerated for 1–2 days. They are best eaten as soon as they reach full ripeness. Their flavour is most intense when eaten at room temperature or just slightly chilled.

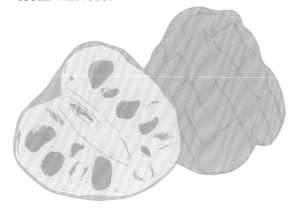

Grapes

If you ever meet a viticulturist - someone who grows grapes, not vitamins - ask them how they care for their vines. Grapes are one of the most heavily sprayed crops going (they're in the dirty dozen; the Environmental Working Group's list of the most pesticide residue-d fruit and veg). Chemical residues don't wash off, so choose organic. It's what the Ancient Greeks ate, and look at all the clever stuff they did.

VEGETARIAN
Dreamy Grape & Feta Couscous
....

Pop a lidded frying pan over medium heat. Add the couscous, garlic and olive oil. Toast for a min.

Add a pinch of salt and pepper. Remove from the heat. Pour enough water over the couscous to just cover it. Stir. Put a lid on the pan. Leave till the water is absorbed, about 10 mins.

Uncover. Add a pinch of chilli, cinnamon and a good squeeze of lemon juice and zest.

Fold in the grapes and the mint. Dot with feta. Sprinkle with almonds and more mint. Gorgeous with roast lamb.

> ♡ **Grapes love...**
>
> Feta, blue cheese, brie, goat's cheese, partridge, pheasant, pigeon, lamb, mint, tarragon, pinenuts, walnuts.

- ½ mug of couscous
- 1 garlic clove, finely chopped
- A few glugs of olive oil
- Sea salt and freshly ground pepper
- Boiling water
- A pinch of chilli powder
- A pinch of ground cinnamon
- 1 lemon, juice and zest
- 4 large handfuls of grapes (any colour), halved
- 2 large handfuls of fresh mint, chopped
- 200g feta cheese, cut into cubes
- A large handful of almonds, roughly chopped and toasted

Prep: 15 mins
Cook: 10 mins
Serves: 4

A bunch of ideas

Super cool

Frozen grapes, especially red ones, make stunning ice cubes. Drop in a jug of punch or sangria.

Super hot

Bung a few handfuls of grapes in a roasting dish next to a leg of lamb, mutton or game and add a splash of red wine. Green grapes are gorgeous stuffed in the cavity of a roasting chicken. Once cooked, scoop out the grapes and make a sauce using the pan juices, white wine, tarragon and crème fraîche.

Super slush

Whizz up frozen grapes (any colour) in a food processor for a quick sorbet. If needed, add a drop of icing sugar to sweeten.

Super bowl

Make this very quick and easy pudding with frozen grapes. Let them sit at room temp for a few mins before serving, to soften them a tad. Pretty easy, see? Delicious with chocolate truffles.

Pears

If you swing by our office in the morning, you'll hear our lunch club chef, Paul, chirpily singing along to his reggae/punk/beats. Paul creates amazing lunches for us using our left over fruit and veg. Pear & Chilli Mash is one of his greatest hits.

A trio of ideas

Cake bake

Slice or dice your pear and add it to a chocolate cake, brownie or sticky toffee pudding recipe.

A game of halved pears

Lay halved pears, cut side down, in a roasting tray next to pheasant or other game. Add a splosh of red wine, a drizzle of honey and a few sprigs of rosemary. Check often. Remove once toasty and tender.

Icy creamy sherbet

Peel and dice ripe pears. Add a squeeze of lemon to preserve the colour. Freeze. Whip frozen dice in a food processor with vanilla seeds and a dollop of mascarpone.

Storage tips

Pears are fussy little things. They go from under-ripe to over-ripe quicker than you can say crumble. If they're firm when you get them, store at room temp to ripen. Keep an eye on them though, they're shifty little blighters. When they give a little, eat or pop in the fridge.

♡ Pears love...

Saffron, cinnamon, wine, ginger, chamomile, cured meat, game, lamb, clotted cream, sticky toffee pudding.

Pear & Chilli Mash

Gorgeous with roast pork or crispy skinned hake.
Or make it a vegan main with wedges of roast broccoli
and toasted almonds.

Cook spuds so they're mashable: roast whole or peel,
cube and boil in salted water. Mash with a little milk
and butter or olive oil.

Prep your pears and chillies while the spuds cook.
When ready, swirl the pears and chilli through the
mash till everything melds together.

Season well. Add more chilli if needed and a squeeze
of lemon juice. Delicious with a final dab of butter or
a drizzle of olive oil.

- 3 large potatoes
- A little olive oil or butter
- A splash of milk (optional)
- 3 ripe pears, cored, peeled
  and finely diced
- 1 chilli, deseeded, finely
  chopped (to taste)
- Sea salt and freshly
  ground pepper
- 1 lemon, juice

Prep: 15 mins

Cook: 30 mins–1 hr (depends
on how you cook the spuds)

Serves: 4

Plums

Knocking back Serbian plum brandy (Slivovitz, seeing as you asked) is probably not the best way to get one of your 5 a day. Fresh, organic plums, straight from the fridge? Now you're talking. They're so delicious, so cold and so sweet.

Plum crazy

Roasty plummy saucy pork

Halve and de-stone some plums and bung in a tray alongside a joint of pork. Add a few splashes of soy sauce, some chilli, freshly grated ginger, a cinnamon stick and a pinch of sugar. Cover. Remove plums before the pork if they cook faster. When it's all done, whizz up the fruit and juices to make a sauce.

Savour the salad

Slices of raw plum are super in salad. Especially with Autumn salad leaves, toasted cashews, and the Japanese Dress on page 178.

♡ Plums love...

Honey, pork, star anise, cinnamon, vanilla, cardamom, duck, baked brie.

Sugar plum cakey

Like most fruit, plums are ace in cakes and tray bakes. Once you've poured a classic sponge batter into a tin, press in some halved and de-stoned plums, cut side up. Dust with Demerara sugar and flaked almonds. Bake till set and golden.

Plumge

If you prefer plums skinless, plunge them into boiling water for 30 secs. Remove with a slotted spoon and rinse in cold water before peeling.

Plum Gorgeous Compote

Try this if your plums are a bit soft, or you've got loads.

Roughly chop and remove the stones. Warm in a pan with a good squeeze of citrus. Add vanilla, spices, sugar or honey. Let it bubble up.

Mash with a wooden spoon as it cooks. Taste and add more sweetness or spice, if you fancy. Grate in a little zest. Cook till nice and thick.

If you drag your spoon across the bottom of the pot and the compote separates for a moment, long enough to make a line, it's done.

Serve with ice cream or porridge. Or chill, then layer with yogurt and nuts or granola.

For something more savoury: swap the vanilla for 1 tsp freshly grated ginger and a splash of soy sauce. Add chilli, if you like. Brilliant with duck or slow-roasted pork belly.

- 4–5 ripe plums
- 1 orange, lemon or lime, juice
- ½ vanilla pod, seeds scraped (optional)
- A pinch of ground cinnamon
- 4 whole cloves, or a pinch of ground cloves
- 3–4 tbsp honey or sugar (Demerara is best, but any will do)

Prep: 5 mins

Cook: 20 mins

Serves: 2–4

After the first frost

Nature gives us wonderful things, and they're best when they're free. And when you can mix them with gin.

Sloes are easy to spot. Look for the bluey-plum-dusty-velvet blush of grape-sized fruit on a blackthorn bush.

Sloes can vary in shape and size. They can be elongated and a bit like large grapes, almost like small damsons (similar colour and dustyness). Others are small and round and more like blueberries.

The silver fork

A load of old nonsense, or the secret to sloe success?

Wait till the first frost, then pick and prick your sloes with a silver fork before steeping in gin and sugar.

If there hasn't been a frost, you can freeze your sloes. It's not quite the same, but pretty much does the trick. You can also freeze them if you're not ready to use them, or if you and your mates polished off the gin on Friday, by mistake.

How to turn gin purple

On their own, sloes are so tart they'll turn your face inside out.

In gin, with sugar, they're delicious. Here's how:

Get a pretty glass bottle or two. You'll fill each bottle half full of sloes.

Clean the bottles thoroughly with boiling hot soapy water. Then, pop them in a 100°C/Gas ½ for 5–10 mins to sterilise them.

Wash your sloes and prick them with a sewing needle or silver fork.

Weigh the sloes. Mix them with half their weight in golden caster sugar. So you want 2 parts sloes + 1 part sugar.

Fill your bottles half full with the sugary sloe mixture. Pour enough gin in the bottle to come right to the top.

Repeat till you've used up all of your sloes.

Seal. Shake. Leave till Christmas (or as close as possible). Shake or turn the bottle from time to time to help inject the gin with more colour.

Winter

Frosty noses, knitting, mince pies, roaring fires, boozy Sunday lunches

Neeps and tatties

Winter

Winter starts with the Winter Solstice on 21st or 22nd December. Winter ends on 20th March with the Spring Equinox.

Look out for

Parsnips in December

Blood oranges in January

Roots in February

Kale in March

Things to do in Winter

Build fires

Start a quilting group

Get some new box sets (conversation is overrated when you're all bunged up)

Eat lots of oranges

Collect leaf skeletons

Go on holiday

Love is like a homemade hotpot

There are only three things you really need in Winter, a good pair of socks, a cast iron casserole dish and someone to cuddle.

With a casserole dish, the natural vegetable kingdom is yours.

Slow food rules the roots (and greens, and lamb, and chickpeas, and chicken) in the veg box kitchens of Great Britain.

Winter is... parsnips

There's a very simple reason why parsnips should be eaten in Winter. It's because they taste better.

They're sweeter after the first frost you see, so it's worth the wait.

The other thing to look for in a parsnip is personality. Stay with me.

Some places (not mentioning any names) demand that farmers supply only fruit or veg that fit very specific shape, weight, size and appearance requirements.

Funnily enough, there's not a whisper about flavour in those specifications.

Well, we all know that beauty is skin deep and perfect uniformity isn't natural. It's bonkers to let good food go to waste and sometimes it's the wonkiest parsnip that tastes the best.

Clementine parsnips

Black salsify

What's brown and sticky? A brown stick.

Not to be mistaken for a twig, black salsify are wily; they look unassuming yet their delicate flavour evokes potatoes, parsnips, even oysters.

Salsify has sap which can stick to your pan if you peel it before boiling. Leave it on and it'll rub off easily once boiled.

> ♡ **Salsify loves...**
>
> Lemon, roast chicken, pan fried white fish, white wine, Parmesan, black pepper, parsley, chilli, bacon, chorizo.

Twiggy tips

Chilli Parmesan pieces

Cut your sticks into 3–4 cm bits and boil for 15–25 mins (the bigger the bits, the longer it'll take). Rub or peel off the skin. In a little oil, fry the garlic and chilli (powder or fresh) till they pick up colour. Serve with freshly grated Parmesan. Or branch out and wrap them in filo pastry and bake.

Bacon branches

Sizzle peeled, thinly sliced salsify with bits of smoky bacon, a finely chopped onion or leek, rosemary or thyme and a splash of oil. Season. Once golden and tender, finish with lots of pepper and a dollop of crème fraîche if you have any.

Storage tips

Even though they look like they might be at home propping up your beans, store your sticks in the fridge. See a picture of them on page 241.

Easy pan pipes

Peel, rinse and cut into chunks. Fry in a hot pan with butter, salt and pepper. When they're golden, add a splash of wine or stock to soften. Then choose a cuisine to suit your mood. Try a scattering of rosemary or thyme, a shake of Indian spices or some fresh ginger, chilli, lime juice, honey and soy sauce.

Javelin gratin

Peel, chop and fry for a bit. Cover in a creamy sauce (a little wine reduced down with the salsify, some crème fraîche or cream and grated Parmesan). Pop in a baking dish. Top with cheese or breadcrumbs and a scattering of nuts and/or herbs. Bake till golden and tender.

Brussels sprouts

I love Brussels sprouts. Absolutely adore them. Although I'm not alone, I know that some people disagree with me. I reckon that anyone can love sprouts. You've just got to know what to do with them...

Tiny cabbage inspiration

Criss cross

It's popular to make a criss cross in the base of sprouts, but we prefer halving or quartering. They cook quicker this way and absorb more flavours.

Shreddies

Shred your sprouts (cut them into thin slices) and pan-fry them with the things they love. Shredded sprouts are also fab in a stir-fry.

Big bang theory

Sprouts like to lap up big, bold flavours. A Parmesan and smoky bacon combo is the ultimate. Shred or quarter your sprouts. Sizzle your bacon in a little oil till golden. Add the sprouts and a drop of water. Fry till glossy and green. Crumble in some chestnuts if you have any. Season with lots of black pepper. Finish with a little Parmesan. Badda bing, badda bang.

Storage tips

Keep sprouts in a paper bag in the fridge. Strip off the tatty leaves (save them for stock) before cooking.

Cumin Brussels Sprouts

Strip off any sad-looking outer leaves if necessary. Halve or quarter your sprouts, depending on their size.

Sit a wok or frying pan over a high heat. Dry toast the cumin for a mo. Add the butter. Let it froth up a little.

Put the sprouts, a good pinch of salt, pepper and lemon zest in the pan. Cook for a couple of mins till the sprouts start to soften.

Add 2–3 tbsp of water. Let it sizzle till it almost evaporates. Your sprouts should be bright green, crisp and tender, with a silky butter sauce. Squeeze in a good bit of lemon juice. Taste. Adjust seasoning, if needed. Serve.

- 1 tsp cumin seeds
- 50g butter
- 800g Brussels sprouts
- Sea salt and freshly ground pepper
- 1 lemon, juice and zest

Prep: 10 mins
Cook: 10 mins
Serves: 4–6

Cabbage

Whether it's a January king, a sweetheart or a savoy cabbage (and so on), these bold, brave brassicas keep us in greens in the Winter months.

Cabbage is totally underrated, in my humble opinion. Probably because not everyone knows how very versatile they are.

Bowling green

Smoke gets in your fries

Finely shred your cabbage. Snip some smoked bacon into pieces. Fry till golden. Stir the cabbage with a little splash of oil and cook till tender. Add some chestnuts or grated apple, or both.

Marvellous as a side dish or mixed through steaming pasta. It adds a bit of punch to a bowl of vegetable soup too.

Nicey spicy

Cabbage loves a bit of spice, particularly cumin. Finely chop and sizzle in some oil with garlic and a pinch of cumin seeds. If cumin's not your thing, try fresh chilli, ginger and a swish of soy sauce.

Add a splash of water. Cook till tender, glossy and luscious green. Delicious with roast lamb or lemony chickpeas.

> ♡ **Cabbage loves...**
>
> Cumin, caraway seeds, pork, bacon, cheddar, anchovies, balsamic vinegar, ginger, chilli, soy sauce, potatoes, beer, sage, chestnuts, apple.

Dial-A-Cabbage Wedges

Preheat the oven to 200°C/Gas 6.

Cut your cabbage into quarters or about six chunky wedges. Slice through the stem and keep it in so the wedges stay intact. Crush the garlic cloves with the side of a knife. Remove the peel.

Warm your stock in a saucepan.

Sizzle the wedges in a large frying pan with a little butter or oil, garlic and a few sage or bay leaves, if you fancy. Season. Once the wedges are lightly golden on each cut side, nestle them in a roasting tin along with the garlic and herbs.

Pour the stock over the wedges. Roast for about 20–25 mins. The cabbage should be tender all the way through. Amazing with bangers and mash.

- 1 head of green cabbage like savoy
- 3 garlic cloves
- 500ml veg or chicken stock
- A good splash of olive oil or a little butter
- Sea salt and freshly ground pepper
- A few sage or bay leaves (optional)

Prep: 5 mins
Cook: 30 mins
Serves: 4–6

Emma's Cabbage in a Pasta
· ·

When our Emma makes this, she adjusts the recipe depending on what greens she's got. Hardy cabbages need a longer steam, while pak choi, spinach and chard only need a brief steam. Or you can skip steaming, and pop them in with the pasta for a few mins before you drain it all. Saves on washing up, and does the job nicely.

Boil pasta till al dente. Pre-steam your cabbage or greens, if needed. Once the pasta is cooked, add the greens, stir, then drain immediately.

As the pasta cooks, mix the anchovies (with the oil from their tin), garlic, juice of half a lemon and chilli. Cook till the anchovies disintegrate. Add a little more oil or some butter, if needed, to make it loose enough to fold through the cabbage and pasta.

Fold the sauce through. Taste. Adjust seasoning and lemon juice as needed.

Serve with crackings of pepper and lashings of Parmesan, to taste.

- 400g spaghetti
- 1 green cabbage or a bag of greens, finely shredded
- A glug of olive oil
- 50g tin of anchovies, plus the oil
- 1 lemon, juice
- 3–4 garlic cloves, finely chopped
- A pinch of chilli flakes or chilli powder
- Sea salt and freshly ground pepper
- A large handful of freshly grated Parmesan

Prep: 10 mins
Cook: 15 mins
Serves: 4

Abel & Colecannon

. . . .

This is our take on the classic Irish dish made with kale or cabbage and spuds. For the Abel-ified version you can chuck in all sorts of greens and root veg.

It's great with British free range pork sausages and/or roasted tomatoes, garlic and red peppers.

Peel and cut your spuds and roots into chunks (the smaller they are, the faster they'll cook). Boil in lightly salted water.

Meanwhile, rinse and thinly slice your greens. Steam or gently fry in a little oil till tender. Season to taste.

When they're soft enough to mash, drain the spuds and roots. Mash. Swirl in crème fraîche, butter, milk, and/or oil so it's just how you like it.

Stir fresh thyme leaves, a little mustard, some black pepper, a touch of lemon and freshly grated Parmesan through your mash. All these are optional so use whatever you have to hand. Taste as you go.

Swirl in the softened greens and it's ready.

If you're vegan, swap the dairy products for a little olive oil, extra lemon juice and add a touch of chilli powder.

- 6 handfuls of root veg and spuds (half and half works well)
- 2–3 handfuls of Wintry greens (leeks, kale, cabbage, etc)
- A splash of olive oil
- A bit of crème fraîche, butter, milk or olive oil
- A few sprigs of thyme, leaves only
- A hit of Dijon mustard
- Freshly ground pepper
- 1 lemon, juice (optional)
- Freshly grated Parmesan (optional)

Prep: 10 mins

Cook: 30 mins

Serves: 4

Storage tips

Keep cabbage in the fridge. It doesn't freeze well unless it's been cooked into a batch of colcannon.

Red cabbage

Red cabbage is gorgeous and boy does it go far. It has an uncanny way of almost doubling in volume when you slice it up, so it's great if you owe a few people supper.

Cabbage creations

Amazing braisings

Braising is the ultimate way to shift red cabbage and there are loads of variations. Our favourite twist is to mull it with spice and wine, as on the right. For an Italian job: swap the wine for balsamic vinegar and toss in toasted hazelnuts, fresh parsley and lemon zest at the end. Or try water instead of wine and, at the end, a good swish of soy sauce, freshly grated ginger, chilli, garlic and fresh coriander.

Cabbage crunch kids

Raw red cabbage is rawfully nice, especially in coleslaw. A traditional mayo coleslaw works well, even though it'll go a little pink. Or try an Asian twist (citrus juice, fresh ginger, chilli, toasted cashews, coriander, soy sauce and honey). Or take inspiration from Italy with balsamic vinegar, orange juice, crispy Parma ham, sage and Parmesan.

And now for something...

A little bit different: roasted whole red cabbage leaves. Start by peeling off the leaves. Lightly coat them in oil (use a brush or shake and turn them in the baking tray). Arrange in a single layer on a baking tray. Dust with salt and pepper then roast till crisp and toasty.

Storage tips

If it's cold in your kitchen you can get away with leaving your cabbage out of the fridge. It keeps better stored whole. Once cut, definitely keep it in the fridge and use fairly quickly.

VEGAN

Mulled Red Cabbage

Delicious as it is, braised red cabbage is a bit run of the mill. This is a bit more run of the mull.

Over a low heat, add a splash of olive oil to a heavy-based pot. When hot, add the spices and bay. Stir.

Add the cabbage, a grating of clementine and lemon zest, the clementine juice, sugar and half a mug of wine.

Cover and simmer over a very low heat for about an hour. Stir now and again. Add more wine if needed, so it doesn't dry out or catch at the bottom.

After an hour, uncover. Turn up the heat. Splash in more wine, little by little, letting it guzzle it up like risotto. Taste. The cabbage should be dark, glossy and sweet. Season as needed.

Finish with a squeeze of lemon juice and a little more zest. It's worth noting that you can make this dish a day or two in advance, and just gently reheat it. It freezes well.

- A splash of olive oil
- 1 cinnamon stick
- 8 cloves
- 2 bay leaves
- ½ large red cabbage, finely shredded, white core removed
- 2 clementines, juice and zest
- ½ lemon, juice and zest
- 2 tbsp Demerara sugar
- 1 mug of red wine
- Sea salt and freshly ground pepper

Prep: 10 mins

Cook: 1 hr

Serves: 6

Cauliflower

Beautiful snowy cauliflower. Like a vegetable cloud resting in a big green cup. Great in curry (see page 91), broken up and roasted with oil and Indian spices, or stir-fried with Asian flavours. Or raw, like in this 'ere pretty dish.

VEGAN OR VEGETARIAN
Cauliflower Couscous

A brilliant way to shift a whole head of cauliflower is to turn it into couscous. Seriously. A lovely light lunch on its tod, or with a green salad. A superb supper with pan-fried fish, or nuggets of warm chorizo. (Keep the leaves and stalk for stir-fries or soup.)

Toast the nuts or seeds in a dry frying pan. Once golden and fragrant, drizzle in a little honey to gloss. Let it sizzle a bit so it coats the nuts or seeds with a sticky, caramel glaze. Add a little olive oil to keep the honey from clumping too much. Set aside.

Whizz up the cauli and garlic in a food processor till it looks like couscous. No whizzy gadgets? Just chop the florets as finely as you can.

Mix the spices together. Fold through the cauli. Gloss with olive oil and a splash of vinegar. Add some citrus zest and juice, herbs and the nuts or seeds.

Taste. Add a touch more vinegar, citrus, oil or salt, if needed.

> ### Storage tips
> Keep cauli in the fridge.

- 100g chopped almonds, pinenuts or other seeds
- 1–2 tbsp honey or agave syrup
- A splash of olive oil
- 1 head of cauliflower florets roughly chopped
- 1 plump garlic clove
- 1 tsp paprika
- 1 tsp ground cumin
- 1 tsp ground coriander
- ½ tsp ground cinnamon
- ½ tsp ground ginger
- A pinch of chilli powder
- A splash of cider vinegar
- 1 orange or lemon, juice and zest
- 2 handfuls of fresh mint, parsley and/or coriander, chopped
- Sea salt

Prep: 10 mins
Cook: 5 mins
Serves: 2–4

♡ Cauliflower loves...

Walnuts, blue cheese, chilli, cumin, coriander, chorizo, bacon, cream, Parmesan, cheddar, almonds, sherry.

Celeriac

It may have been hit by the ugly stick, but that's no reason not to fall in love with the big lump of veg that is celeriac.

Once you peel off its rough skin you're left with creamy, ivory flesh that hints of celery and apple.

Celeriac selectors

Low carbon celeriac

Raw's the way forward. Grated celeriac is lovely raw in salads with mayo-esque dressings or cut into batons and dipped into a pot of pesto. Tasty.

Soft celeriac

Celeriac makes wicked soup, especially if you involve blue cheese. Fry a chopped onion in butter or oil till soft. Add peeled, cubed celeriac and chopped garlic. Season. Fry it for a few mins, crack in a bit of salt and pepper.

Pour in some stock, to just cover the veg. Simmer. When it's softened whizz it up. Add a bit more stock if needed. Swirl in the cheese so it melts. Done.

Alottorisotto

Fry an onion. Once it's softened, add small cubes of peeled celeriac and risotto rice. Cook for a few mins. Add a glass of wine. Ladle in some stock slowly, so the liquid keeps reducing as the rice swells. Stir frequently. When the rice doesn't need any more liquid (see Casanova's Celery Risotto, page 75, for measurements), add some mascarpone, shredded ham and another spoon of stock. Stir till creamy. Finish with fresh herbs and lemon juice.

Step away from the peeler

A veg peeler is no match for celeriac. Use a sturdy knife instead. Make an incision with just the tip of your knife, carefully and gradually cutting small panels or wedges out of the veg. Carve the skin from each slice.

See page 223 for our celeriac chip tip.

Cheery Winter Waldorf

Put this in a sandwich or add leafy greens to make an uplifting salad. It's also absolutely delicious with cold or warm roast chicken.

Mix the celeriac and apple in a bowl along with the lemon juice and zest. Season well.

Fold in the garlic and crème fraîche or mayo. Scatter over your rocket or herbs (or both if you want) and the roast chicken or nuts. Give it all a gentle mix, then serve.

> ♡ Celeriac loves...
>
> Game, crème fraîche, parsley, Parmesan, roast pork, black pepper, garlic, mustard, pear, salmon, cheddar.

- 2 mugs of celeriac (or parsnips), peeled and cut into matchsticks
- 2 mugs of apples, cut into matchsticks
- 1 lemon, juice and zest
- Sea salt and freshly ground pepper
- 1 garlic clove, finely chopped
- 2 mugs of crème fraîche or 1 mug of mayo
- A big handful of herbs or rocket
- A handful of toasted pinenuts, walnuts or cold roast chicken (optional)

Prep: 10 mins

Cook: nil

Serves: 2–4

Celery

Sticks of celery are useful for safety-conscious fencing enthusiasts or for propping up tiny bio-degradable tents when you're playing imaginary mini-Glastonbury at home.

Nececelery tips

Great gratin

Layer thinly sliced celery with wispy slices of potato, cheese, a little cream and a bit of stock. Top with breadcrumbs, nuts and herbs. Bake till golden.

Moondance

For something to rave about, mix up thin celery moons with orange segments, fresh basil or parsley, and toasted pinenuts.

Breaded moon

Slice celery into thin moons and sit on bread in the following combos: celery and blue cheese with toasted walnuts. Celery, orange zest, honey and a little goat's cheese. Celery, finely grated Parmesan and black olives.

Rocking stock star

Celery is the key to a well-rounded stock. It's equally grand as the main soup ingredient, with roast chestnuts and stilton.

Storage tips

Celery goes bendy if it's not kept in the fridge or in a glass of water on the side. It'll go soggy if you freeze it, but if you've got a glut, make a batch of veg stock with a bunch of other veg peelings and off cuts and freeze that.

♡ Celery loves...

Peanut butter, blue cheese, rice, potatoes, parsley, thyme, citrus, almonds, hazelnuts, chestnuts, caraway seeds, apple.

Casanova's Celery Risotto

The secret to Casanova's wooing power was not his good looks, it was his love of celery. Ok, so maybe a celery farmer made this up, but we've turned a few people on to the stunning stalk with this irresistible risotto.

Place a large pot over medium heat. Add a splash of olive oil. Once hot, gently sauté the onion for 10–15 mins.

Add the risotto rice and let it crackle in the pan for a few mins. Splash in the wine. Let it bubble away till the rice absorbs it all.

Stir in the celery. Add a good grind of pepper and cook for a couple of mins before adding the first ladle of stock.

Set a timer for 20 mins and feed the stock to the rice, little by little, till the timer goes off.

Fold in the mascarpone and a good pinch of salt. Add a tiny bit more stock, if needed. Your risotto should be nice and creamy and not too thick.

Stir in half the herbs and half the Parmesan. Dish up and divvy out the remaining Parmesan and herbs. Finish with a generous crack of black pepper and a crunch of almonds.

- 1 onion, finely chopped
- A splash of olive oil
- 1 mug of risotto rice
- 1 mug of white wine
- 1 mug of celery, finely diced
- 1 ltr chicken or veg stock, simmering
- ½ mug of mascarpone cheese
- Sea salt and freshly ground pepper
- ½ mug of freshly grated Parmesan
- 2 handfuls of Summer herbs (sorrel, basil, tarragon, and/or mint)
- A small handful of toasted almond slivers (optional)

Prep: 10 mins
Cook: 35 mins
Serves: 4

Chicory

The Campari of vegetables, bittory chicory is the most sophisticated Winter lettuce around.

Quick chics

Dippory chicory

Quarter raw chicory lengthways into skinny wedges and dip into a blue cheese dressing, a tangy vinaigrette or houmous.

Chic winter salad

Let the leaves star in a salad with orange segments and pomegranate seeds. Add a crumble of blue cheese, toasted walnuts and a drizzle of honey.

VEGETARIAN
Bitter Sweet Chicory

This gorgeous bitter-sweet recipe is stunning, especially if you like burnt caramel.

Halve your chicory lengthways. Carve out the smooth little triangle bit of white in the centre – removing it helps the chicory cook more evenly.

Get a smallish frying pan quite hot. Add the butter. Let it froth.

Add your chicory halves, cut-side down. Season.

Let them cook for a min. Then add the orange juice (it should come about half way up the chicory). Let it bubble up for a mo, lower the heat, then cover till it's soft and tender.

Uncover and drizzle in the honey or agave. Crank up the heat. Let the liquid reduce down to a thick, toffee-like syrup. The cut-side of the chicory should be nicely golden.

Arrange in a dish. Chuck some herbs over the top and serve. Amazing with fish or Puy lentils, or both.

- 2–4 chicory
- 2–3 tbsp butter
- Sea salt and freshly ground pepper
- 1 mug of orange juice
- 2–3 tbsp honey or agave syrup
- A handful of parsley, chervil or coriander, to serve (optional)

Prep: 5 mins
Cook: 20 mins
Serves: 2–4

Jerusalem artichokes

These knobbly little critters look like the love child of a potato and a ginger root. They're actually related to sunflowers and have nothing to do with the WI.

Artichoke smartichoke

Asian twist

Thinly sliced, raw Jerusalem artichokes are a bit like water chestnuts. They're brilliant in salads or slipped into a stir-fry right at the end.

Mish mash

Peel. Cut into chunks and boil with an equal amount of spuds till tender. Mash with butter, salt, pepper, a little grated nutmeg and Parmesan.

Layer bake

Most roots are fab in a gratin. These beauts love a splash of whisky in the gratin cream. Top with toasted hazelnuts or pinenuts.

Ahem

Some people find these little roots give them a case of the trouser coughs. Some are more affected than others. The more sensitive you are, the more likely you'll be to put an F at the beginning of their name.

> **Storage tips**
> Keep them bagged and refrigerated for up to one week. Scrub well (no need to peel) before cooking.

Jerusalem Artichoke & Hazelnut Soup

Pop butter and oil (just use oil if you want) into a pot with a wide bottom. Place over medium heat. When the butter foams, add the onions. Sizzle slowly till golden.

Add the Jerusalem artichokes and garlic. Cover. Turn heat down. Sweat till really soft. Stir often.

Bung in the sherry and nuts and let it sizzle a bit. Add the thyme and stock. Blitz. When smooth, check the seasoning. Pass through a fine mesh sieve for a silkier consistency. Serve with a little cream, if you like.

♡ Jerusalem artichokes love...

Goat's cheese, hazelnuts, almonds, pinenuts, orange, lemon, soy sauce, cream, Parmesan, nutmeg, thyme.

- 1 tbsp butter and 1 tbsp olive oil
- 1 large onion, finely chopped
- 400g Jerusalem artichokes (8–10 bigger ones), scrubbed clean and thinly sliced
- 2 garlic cloves, finely chopped
- A splash of sherry, Marsala or apple juice
- 4 tbsp hazelnuts or almonds, toasted and ground
- A few sprigs of thyme, leaves only
- 600ml chicken or veg stock, warmed
- A drizzle of cream (optional)

Prep: 10 mins

Cook: 25 mins

Serves: 2

Kale & Cavolo nero

Opportunity knocks when you've got a big bag of seasonal greens in your fridge. Crispy curly kale and velvety cavolo nero are delicious, accommodating and damn healthy to boot.

Green designs

Iron mash

Kale and cavolo nero are loaded with iron. Chop the leaves finely, like parsley and swirl through potato or root mash.

Pan pals

These greens love garlic and chilli (fresh or powdered). With these friends, they need little else. Chop and fry in a splash of oil till bright and glossy. Taste, season and swirl through pasta.

Go bowling

Kale's great in soups or stews. Try chicken noodle soup, a beany soup or stew, hearty veg soup or a spicy sausage hotpot. Finely chop and stir in at the end.

Hey presto!

Both these greens make great pesto. Mosey on over to page 186 for the recipe.

Hakuna frittata

These guys are magical in frittata, omelette or scrambled eggs. See our frittata recipe on page 122.

Cavolo hero

The dark, dreamy leaves of cavolo nero are naturally deep in flavour. All you need do is steam them and gloss with a little olive oil or butter.

> ### Storage tips
> Keep your greens in the fridge washed and wrapped in cloth. If you forget about them, just trim off any yellow bits.

VEGAN
Crispy Kale Seaweed

Inhale a whole bag of curly kale with this Chinese inspired number.

Preheat your oven to 220°C/Gas 7.

Pull the kale leaves from the stalks. Hold the end of the stalk and slide your other hand down toward the leaves, pulling them from the stem as you go.

Finely chop the leaves. Drizzle over a little oil. Toss to coat. Dust with salt, sugar and paprika.

Arrange in a single layer on an ovenproof tray or dish. Bake for about 5 mins (check after 2–3 mins) till still green yet crispy.

• A few handfuls of kale
• A drizzle of olive or sunflower oil
• A pinch of sea salt
• A pinch of caster sugar
• A pinch of paprika (optional)

Prep: 5 mins
Cook: 5 mins
Serves: 2–4

PIZZA the ACTION

VEGAN OR VEGETARIAN
PAN PIZZA

This is a really quick, cheaty and delicious way to make pizza from scratch. It makes 4, and if you've got 4 pans, you can make them all in one go!

Tip flour, baking powder, salt and olive oil into a large mixing bowl. Gently warm the wine. Add. Mix in the warm wine till it forms a dough.

Gently knead till you have a smooth ball. Dust in more flour if needed.

Divide your dough into 2 or 4 pieces, depending on how many pizzas you want. Roll out, dust with flour as needed. Once round and the size-ish of your pans, dust the top with flour and fold in half. Dust again and halve again so you have a triangle.

Brush your pans with oil. Lay the dough in one corner and unfold. Curl sides inward to form the crust. Gloss with oil. Let the base crisp up over medium-low heat while you make the topping.

Heat your grill to high. If you don't have a grill, set your oven to 220°C/Gas 7.

Mix tinned toms with the garlic and balsamic vinegar, fresh rosemary and pepper.

When the pizza bottoms are nicely browned all over, take off the heat. Dollop and spread on your sauce, add the veg and cheese.

Grill till the cheese is golden and bubbly.

*The wine adds heaps of flavour but the recipe will work fine with warm water instead.

For the dough:
- 2 mugs of plain white flour
- 2 tsp baking powder
- A good pinch of sea salt
- 6 tbsp olive oil
- 2/3 mug of white wine*

For the sauce:
- 1 tin of chopped tomatoes
- 1 garlic clove, finely minced
- 1 tbsp balsamic vinegar
- A good pinch of fresh herbs (rosemary is nice), finely chopped
- Sea salt and freshly ground pepper
- Chopped veggies from your box (red pepper, broccoli, tomatoes, courgettes, onions...)
- Cheese to grate or dot over the top (buffalo mozzarella, goat's cheese, cheddar...)

Prep: 15 mins
Cook: 15 mins
Makes: 4 individual pizzas or 2 larger ones

Takeaway pizza will be a thing of the past with this slice of cookery action. This recipe may look long, but when you've done it once, it's a doddle.

The great thing about veg are that they're accommodating. Bulk them out with a few well chosen carbs, and you can make that veg box go really quite far.

EASY PAN PIZZA

OUR FAVOURITE TOPPING TIPS

Caramelised red onions, goat's cheese, broccoli and olives.

Buffalo mozzarella, fresh pesto (see page 186), fresh tomatoes and basil.

Courgette ribbons, thinly sliced onions, marjoram, lemon zest and capers.

Leftover boiled new potatoes (sliced), red pepper slices, rosemary and cheddar.

Really though, you can chuck on whatever you fancy.

You can freeze this pizza dough or the cooked bases (topped or untopped). Just pop into the oven from frozen or defrosted.

The sauce freezes well. If you're impatient, freeze it in an ice cube tray for speedy defrosting.

PIZZA the ACTION

Parsnips

Nick from Bagthorpe Farm, who grows various veg for us throughout the year, once said to me 'parsnips are not carrots'. What he meant was, they're not as popular as the omnipotent carrot. Popular schmopular, their trademark creamy, sweet, rooty flavour epitomises Winter eating.

Snip tips

A Winter's treat

Parsnip and Parmesan gratin is a stunning meat free main. Peel and thinly slice your parsnips. Fry the slices in a little oil or butter till just tender. Season. Layer in a buttered dish, dust with grated Parmesan and freshly ground black pepper. Pour in a mix of cream, milk and a little Dijon mustard till the slices are just covered. Top with breadcrumbs, crushed or flaked almonds and grated nutmeg. Bake till golden and tender.

Crispy snips

For amazing crisps, get a pot of sunflower oil on a high heat. Use a veg peeler to shave off long strands. Add to the oil in small batches. Remove with a slotted spoon. Dust with a little salt for that salty-sweet moreishness.

Saving bacon

Parsnips are delicious in stews and risottos, and great with bacon. Just dice the veg – small for risotto, bigger for soup. Follow your favourite recipe and sizzle the bacon at the onion stage, and add parsnips a bit later.

Storage tips

Parsnips can go bendy quite quickly. Pop them in the fridge to prevent this. Chilled and snug in a paper bag, they should keep for a week or so.

♡ Parsnips love...

Bacon, mascarpone, rosemary, thyme, orange, ginger, chilli, cinnamon, honey, Parmesan, mustard, venison.

Caramelised Parsnips with Clementines & Spice

Roasted parsnips are gorgeous, but they take bloody ages. This is the quick route to parsnip heaven.

Heat a splash of oil in a large frying pan over medium heat. Once the oil is hot, add the parsnips.

Coat them in the oil and cover the pan. Lower the heat. Cook till the parsnips are tender, 10–15 mins.

Remove the lid and continue to cook till golden.

Add the honey or agave, clementine juice and zest, ginger and chilli. Sizzle till the juice reduces down to a sticky glaze.

Season. Taste. Adjust seasoning as needed. Serve.

- 1.5kg parsnips, peeled and cut into chunky batons
- A few glugs of rapeseed, olive or sunflower oil
- Sea salt and freshly ground pepper
- 4 clementines, juice and zest
- A drizzle of honey or agave syrup
- 2 cm slice of fresh ginger, chopped or grated
- A pinch of fresh chilli or chilli powder

Prep: 10 mins

Cook: 20 mins

Serves: 4

Radicchio

The days are short (and your propensity to do much other than hibernate, shorter) so there's every reason to let a little Winter salad put a spring in your step.

Rad ideas

Radicallio raw

Finely chop your purple lettuce. Pair with a sweet and tangy balsamic or red wine vinegar dressing. Throw in bits of blue cheese, slices of ripe pear, toasted hazelnuts and herbs.

Turn up the heat

Quarter your radicchio then shred the leaves. Fry in a little oil, butter and seasoning. Add a splash of balsamic vinegar right at the end, just as the leaves start to cook down and go nicely tender. Gorgeous with freshly cooked pasta, Parma ham and Parmesan.

The name of the game

Radicchio is fantastic with partridge, pigeon or pheasant. Wash and season your bird. Brown all over in a casserole dish or ovenproof frying pan with a little butter and oil. Add shredded radicchio leaves, salt and pepper, a lump of butter, a drop of honey and red wine.

Roast for 20 mins at 220°C/Gas 7, till the bird is just cooked through. Finish with fresh rosemary or thyme, or crispy fried sage leaves.

> ♡ **Radicchio loves...**
> Blue cheese, toasted nuts, game, venison, balsamic vinegar, oxtail, shin of beef, parsley, orange.

Storage tips

Keep radicchio in the fridge. Otherwise you'll have a shrinking violet on your hands (boom, boom).

Composting 101

Each year an estimated 8.3 million tonnes of food is thrown away by UK homes. This costs the average family £680 a year. Absolutely bonkers.

Most food can be eaten, and for the bits that can't, employ some friendly worms.

Composting with earthworms (vermicompost) turns organic waste into very high quality compost, which is a nutrient rich plant food.

You don't have to have a garden to keep a wormery, and it's a good way to make friends with any garden-owning neighbours. It's also a great way to keep 20,000 pets in a small space.

They're efficient as well, converting up to their own weight of waste into half that amount of compost in a day. The technical term for it is casting. (But it's basically poo.)

If you have a wormery, or are thinking of getting one, this is what can go in it:

Vegetable peelings

Egg shells - worms need calcium so egg shells provide this and keep the bin from getting too acidic

Coffee grounds and tea bags

Cereals, minus milk

Fruit

Annual weeds (not seed heads)

Tomatoes

Bread

Green leaves

Secrets of a wormery

Worms get bored so don't give them too much of one thing.

Don't add too much citrus peel, meat or fish scraps.

Rabbit, dog and cat hairs can be wormerised.

Wait for the worms to tuck into the last lot before adding more waste.

Don't let the bin get too hot or too dry.

Mix in shredded cardboard from time to time so it doesn't get too wet.

The end product (no pun intended) is an excellent fertiliser for your veg. Use as a top dressing, or make your own potting compost using 25% worm casts as the base. Mix liquid feed using one part feed with ten parts water.

A worm composter needs a little TLC - but it's heaps better than chucking stuff in the bin.

All the roots

There's a fair amount of common sense in seasonal eating. In Winter we harvest roots, which is good timing as we need the carbs to keep the chill out.

Parsnips, carrots, swede, Jerusalem artichokes, turnips, beetroot, celeriac, sweet potatoes and regular spuds are uncomplicated creatures and you can choose any or all for these recipes.

Jazzy Roast Roots

Pop your roasting tin in the oven when you preheat it to 200°C/Gas 6. Cut your veg into good-sized pieces (think golf balls) as they shrink when they cook. Season and coat in oil. Tumble into the hot tin and cook till golden. Check and shake the pan every 15 mins or so. They'll take about an hour. And then...

Pick your favourite flavours

Japanese lessons

Grate some fresh ginger over your hot roots as soon as you take them out of the oven. Drizzle over a bit of soy sauce and honey. Scatter on some toasted sesame seeds, fresh coriander or basil.

Middle East feast

Pile warm roasted roots into pitta bread with houmous. Top with a dollop of yogurt and fresh mint or salad.

Health food shop

Toss roasted roots into a batch of freshly made bulgar wheat or couscous. Dress with herbs, toasted seeds and lots of lemon juice and zest.

Storage tips

Roots are fine out of the fridge for a couple of days if your room is cardigan wearing temperature. If you've got a warm kitchen, put them in the fridge.

Roots Manoeuvre Curry

This is one of our most popular recipes. You can shift a load of veg and it's surprisingly easy (don't be put off by the length). Try 3 or 4 roots and any other veg you have kicking around.

Preheat the oven to 200°C/Gas 6. Pop a large roasting tin in the oven to heat up; roots need room to crisp.

In a bowl, coat your chopped roots with oil and some salt and pepper. When the pan is hot, add the veg. Shake to distribute evenly. Roast for 45 mins.

Toast the cumin, coriander and fennel seeds in a dry frying pan for a min or two, till fragrant. Grind to a rough powder. Mix in the turmeric. Set aside.

Put the onion, garlic, chilli and ginger in a blender and purée.

Over medium-low temp, heat a splash of oil in a pan and fry the ground spices for a min. Add the onion paste. Stir frequently for about 5 mins. You want the paste soft, fragrant and reduced in volume. Add more oil, if needed.

Stir in the tomatoes, coconut milk and cinnamon. Simmer, stir constantly. Season. Pour the sauce over the roasting veg and add any softer veg like cauliflower or greens, if using.

Bake uncovered for 20 mins. When the roots are tender and the sauce thick, it's done.

Finish with lime juice and fresh coriander leaves. Gorgeous with basmati rice, a dollop of yogurt or toasted cashews.

- A few good splashes of oil
- 6 large handfuls of root veg, peeled and diced (3–4 cm)
- 2 heaped tsp cumin seeds
- 2 heaped tsp coriander seeds
- 1 heaped tsp fennel seeds
- 2 tsp ground turmeric
- 1 large onion, roughly chopped
- 4 large garlic cloves, roughly chopped
- 1 green chilli, roughly chopped (to taste)
- A thumb-sized piece of fresh ginger, roughly chopped
- 1 tin of chopped tomatoes
- 1 tin of coconut milk
- 2 cinnamon sticks
- Any other veg you fancy
- A handful of fresh coriander
- 1 lime, juice
- Sea salt and freshly ground pepper

Prep: 20 mins

Cook: 1 hr

Serves: 4–6

Gazza's One Pot Wonder

Delivery driver turned Abel & Cole photographer Gaz is the most wonderfully laid back person on the planet and a fantastic cook.

Preheat the oven to 180°C/Gas 4. Remove the giblets from the bird. (Use them later, along with the bones, to make stock.)

Get a lidded pot that's roomy enough for the bird and the veg to have a bit of space. Cut an onion in half to place under the bird to create a trivet. Sit the chicken on the onion.

Peel (if needed) and roughly chop your veg. Cozy it up in the pot around the chicken. Bung in a few garlic cloves.

Halve your orange or lemon. Squeeze a little juice over the chicken and pop the rest into the cavity.

Add some herbs. If chopped, scatter them over, if whole, tuck them into the pot. Season well. Pour in the wine. Gloss with olive oil.

Cover and bake for an hour.

Uncover. Crank the heat up to 220°C/Gas 7. Let the bird brown for 20–30 mins, till cooked and nicely golden. Test that it's done by piercing the fat part of the leg with a knife. If the juices run clear, it's done.

Let it rest for 30 mins before carving, the longer the better – up to an hour is perfectly suitable. It will stay surprisingly warm.

Accompany with some quickly cooked up seasonal greens and a bottle of your favourite wine.

*If you want to cook a larger chicken, add an extra 5 mins to the cooking time for each 100g added to the weight.

- 1.4kg chicken*
- A few onions and/or leeks
- A few carrots
- Some spuds and root veg (swede, parsnips, anything apart from beetroot – unless you want a pink chick!)
- A few crushed garlic cloves
- 1 orange or lemon, halved
- A handful of rosemary, thyme or a few bay leaves
- A glass of white wine
- Sea salt and freshly ground pepper
- A drizzle of olive oil

Prep: 15 mins
Cook: 1 hr 30 mins
Serves: 4–6

Swede

Swedes, eh? Who'd have thought they'd reach such glamorous heights! Chart toppers innumerable times. Fancy dress parties across the country emulating their 70s style. Meryl Streep singing on top of a cliff. Oh, hang on. Wrong swedes.

Alternative swedes

Hot chip

Pop peeled, chunked swede into sizzling hot oil or fat and roast till golden. Right at the end, coat with freshly chopped sage.

The bee cheese

Quickly fry thin slices of peeled swede in oil, to soften. In a buttered dish, layer with chopped garlic and cheese. Add a mix of cream and milk or stock, enough to moisten the veg. Top with breadcrumbs, cheese and hazelnuts. Bake till golden and bubbly.

Spice girls

Fry peeled and diced swede in a little oil, with a pinch of salt. Cover to speed it up if you like. Throw in pinches of Indian spices like turmeric, mustard seeds, curry leaves, chilli powder, cinnamon, ginger and cloves.

♡ Swede loves...

Crème fraîche, Indian spices, whisky, vanilla, mascarpone, beef, lamb, smoked or meaty roasted fish (like bass), butter, nutmeg, lime, coriander, carrots, spuds.

Smokin' Neeps & Tatties Hash

The perfect one-pan supper to warm your cockles on a chilly January night.

If you're vegan, simply leave out the fish, butter and crème fraîche and replace with extra lemon juice, walnuts, and a bit of chilli, if you like.

In a bowl, toss the veg with a little oil and seasoning. Arrange in a single layer in a hot frying pan, add more oil if necessary. Sizzle for a min or two.

If you're adding haddock, soak it in warm water for 5–10 mins. Drain. Fleck the fish from the skin.

Turn your veg in the pan. Cover till it softens. Uncover. Add a slosh of whisky (if using) and a lump of butter (or more oil). Fold in the garlic, leek and thyme. Cook till nicely coloured. Stir often.

Fold in the fish and lemon juice. Taste. Adjust seasoning. Finish with a dusting of lemon zest and chopped herbs.

Delicious served hot with a dollop of crème fraîche, a thick slice of warm bread, cold butter and a bottle of real ale.

- 4 handfuls of potato, peeled and diced
- 2 handfuls of swede, peeled and diced (or any root: turnip, parsnip, celeriac...)
- A few glugs of olive oil
- Sea salt and freshly ground pepper
- 2–3 smoked haddock fillets (optional)
- 2 garlic cloves, finely chopped
- 1 leek, cleaned and sliced
- A sprig of thyme, leaves only
- A glug of whisky (optional)
- A nugget of butter
- 1 lemon, juice and zest
- A handful of parsley or chervil
- Crème fraîche, to serve

Prep: 15 mins

Cook: 30 mins

Serves: 4–6

Citrus

A kitchen without a lemon is like a market without a farmer, not quite right, but more common than you'd like.

Lemons and limes pop up in recipes throughout this book, so I've focussed on the orange family for these pages. If you have a backlog of lemons and limes you can always make lemonade, limeade, or a round of G&Ts.

VEGETARIAN
15 Min Marmalade
. . . .

A quick route to marmalade heaven.

Juice your fruit. Put 4 tbsp of the juice in a saucepan.

Cut the juiceless outer (peel and pith) into thirds. Cut away any white flesh and pith. Slice remaining rind into thin wisps till you have 2 tbsp. Add to the pan.

Let it bubble up over a medium heat. Stir in the honey with a wooden spoon. When it boils again, reduce the heat and simmer for about 7 mins. Stir the whole time.

That's it. It'll be a bit runny, but will thicken in 30–60 mins. Use straight away or refrigerate for 2–3 months.

- 1–2 oranges
  (or 2–3 clementines)
- 4 tbsp clear honey

Prep: 5–10 mins
Cook: 10 mins
Serves: 4–6 people

Storage tips

Lemons, oranges and limes are fine in the fruit bowl when the weather's cool, which is when they're in season. If you have them kicking around in the hotter months, pop them in the fridge.

Citrus Spotter's Guide

Little oranges

Mandarins

A bit bitter, with pips. Use thick slices to make fruit tea: just add honey and fresh mint.

Clementines

Make a reduction for fish by simmering freshly squeezed juice with butter.

Big oranges

Blood oranges

Tangy and juicy. The flesh is deep red or orange with red streaks. Delicious in salads with grains (like quinoa).

Seville oranges

Bitter but brilliant for marmalade. Use the juice in salad dressings too.

Oranges

Sweet, juicy and seedless. Nothing beats freshly squeezed juice.

Grapefruit

(Not technically an orange.) Often quite tart but juicy. Use instead of lemons in a drizzle cake.

Bwarrk Baked Citrus Chicken

If you've ever popped a whole lemon or orange in the cavity of a chicken before roasting, you'll know that chicken and citrus go very nicely together indeed.

Preheat your oven to 200°C/Gas 6. Pop the chicken in a roasting tray. Gloss with oil and season well.

Tuck the orange segments in amongst the chicken. Roast for 25 mins.

Squeeze the juice from one of the orange segments over the chicken. Drizzle the honey over the chicken and decorate the skin with chilli and garlic.

Crank the oven up to 230°C/Gas 8 and cook for a further 15 mins to crisp the skin.

Add a final squeeze of roasted orange juice over the chicken and finish with a scattering of fresh herbs.

- 4 chicken thighs, 4 drumsticks or 2 legs
- Olive oil
- Sea salt and freshly ground pepper
- 2 oranges, quartered
- 1 red chilli, finely chopped (to taste)
- 3 garlic cloves, finely chopped
- 2 tbsp honey
- A handful of fresh coriander, chervil or parsley, roughly chopped

Prep: 10 mins

Cook: 40 mins

Serves: 2–4

♡ Citrus loves...

Just about anything; quinoa, bulgar wheat, fish, pretty much all meats, butter, sugar, honey, avocado, root veg, mixed spice, rosemary, coriander.

Dates

Just look at that picture. Crikey. That's some seriously hot dates.

VEGETARIAN
Spiced Date Brownie Cake
· ·

This totally fabulous recipe is from Ana Miranda and Abbie Quin, who run The Tartelettes, one of our favourite South London cakeries.

Line a large rectangular baking dish (approx 30 x 24 cm) with baking paper.

In a large saucepan, add the dates, lemon zest, coffee, spices, honey, pomegranate molasses, sugar and butter. Simmer and stir till combined. Let it cool fully.

Preheat your oven to 180°C/Gas 4.

Beat the eggs in a large bowl. Add the flour, baking powder and the cooled coffee/date mix. Chop half the nuts and add them to the mix. Stir everything together.

Pour into the lined dish. Scatter the seeds and remaining nuts evenly over the top.

Bake for an hour, or till a skewer poked in comes out with just a few tiny moist crumbs stuck to it. Cover with a large layer of baking paper or foil after 30 mins, to stop the nuts from burning.

To give it a stunning gloss, warm 4 tbsp of apricot jam till syrupy. Brush over the top.

Once cool, remove from dish and cut into squares. Store in an airtight container. It also freezes well.

*Turn over for a tip on how to make your own molasses, or just swap with black treacle or extra honey.

- 300g stoned dates, finely chopped
- 2 lemons, zest only
- 500ml freshly brewed strong black coffee
- Crushed seeds from 12 cardamom pods
- 2 tsp cinnamon
- 2 tsp mixed spice
- 4 tbsp honey
- 4 tbsp pomegranate molasses*
- 250g dark brown sugar
- 150g unsalted butter
- 3 eggs
- 150g mixed nuts
- 4 tbsp sesame, pumpkin and/or sunflower seeds
- 400g plain wholemeal or spelt flour
- 1 tbsp baking powder
- 4 tbsp apricot jam (optional)

Prep: 30 mins

Cook: 1 hr

Serves: 16–20

♡ **Dates love...**

Natural yogurt, banana, cinnamon, vanilla ice cream, orange, chicory, walnuts, marzipan, chilli, coffee.

Storage tips

Dried dates are fine at room temperature.

Pomegranate

Beautiful, sweet, tangy, delicious and bursting with vits. Pomegranates are the crown jewels of the fruit world. They can be a right pain in the rear if you don't know how to handle them, but in approximately 2 mins you will.

How to get seeds from your pomegranate without painting your kitchen pink

Loosen the seeds first by rolling it on a hard surface (a table, the head of a loved one, a very large domino) pressing a little with the palm of your hand.

Place a sieve over a large bowl. Cut the pomegranate in half over this. It saves your work surface from going pink and it catches the lovely juice. To remove the seeds, give the back of the fruit a whack with a wooden spoon. If that doesn't do the trick, invert the fruit and tease them out with your fingers.

To extract more juice, just squeeze the jewel-like seeds. To make pomegranate molasses (fab in Middle Eastern dishes and the cake on page 102) gently simmer the juice down to a syrup.

Another trick for seed removal is to top and tail the fruit, cut into wedges and coax the seeds out of their little nest.

That's it. Lovely pomegranate juice and seeds without your kitchen looking like a 4 year old girl redecorated it.

♡ Pomegranate loves...

Lamb, pigeon, halloumi, feta, fresh mint, orange, white chocolate, dates, pistachios, figs. It also loves white clothing but it's highly advisable to keep them separate!

Storage tips

These stunners are fine at room temperature and can keep for weeks. The seed pips can be frozen in an airtight bag for up to a year. Fresh juice should be refrigerated; it'll keep for a few days. Or you can freeze it.

Sharon fruit

Also known as persimmon and kaki, this tropical fruit is a bit like a seedless orange tomato, but sweet and fruity. When our English orchards are bare of fruit, Spanish farmers come to the rescue with these tri-monikered marvels. No need to peel, just eat them as you would a plum.

Shuggeshtions
. . . .

Roashted

Give your sharon a little squeeze. If it's firm, roasting is a great option. Halve horizontally or slice. Drizzle over a little honey or agave syrup. Roast till golden. Gorgeous warm with a dollop of cream.

Mrs Whippy

If your fruit is soft and squidgy, whizz them up into a delicious nectarine-like purée. It's heavenly swirled through vanilla yogurt, or dolloped into a steamy bowl of porridge with a dab of honey.

Swoony persalady

These are sweet in salads. Slice horizontally to reveal the sunshine pattern tucked in its centre, a bit like an apple's star. Toss the slices with leaves and a sweet and tangy honeyed balsamic dressing. Add a crumbling of goat's cheese, toasted almonds and fresh herbs.

Salsa, cha cha cha

Guide your sharon into salsa. It's delicious with grilled fish. Dice and mix with lime juice, a splash of cider vinegar, chopped coriander and mint, a touch of chilli powder or chopped fresh red chilli, and a pinch of sugar.

♡ **Sharon fruit loves...**
Honey, goat's cheese, balsamic vinegar, vanilla, yogurt, fresh coriander.

Storage tips

Keep them in the fridge if
they're soft. Leave firmer ones
at room temp till they ripen.

Last Minute Christmas Pudding

We've done away with the need to make a Christmas pudding 16 years in advance. This one can be made on Christmas Eve.

It does need 6 hours soaking, and 6–8 hours steaming, but you don't need to be around for that, and the other bits are a doddle.

Snip the dried fruit into raisin sized pieces (clearly you don't have to do this for the actual raisins). Place the dried fruit into a large bowl. Add sugar, brandy, orange juice and zest, mix well and cover.

Leave for 6 hours or overnight (at room temperature) so the liquid absorbs and the sugar begins to dissolve.

Place the remaining ingredients in a large mixing bowl. Mix thoroughly.

Generously butter a 1 ltr pudding basin. Line the bottom with buttered foil. Add the mixture to the bowl. Cover with a pleated piece of buttered foil (the fold allows for expansion), butter side towards the pudding.

Fold the foil around the rim and tie in place with string so no steam can escape. Make a string handle so you can lift it out of the pan.

Put your pud in a steamer above water or stand on a rack in a saucepan. Add water to the pan, so it comes half way up the pudding basin.

Bring to the boil. Lower the temperature and simmer for 6 hours for a light pudding or 8 hours for a darker one. Check the water occasionally, as it may need topping up.

Let the pudding cool completely. Replace the foil with a new bit. Keep in the fridge or freezer till needed. Thaw completely before reheating.

To reheat the pudding, steam or simmer (in the bowl) in water for about an hour till piping hot. Turn out on to a plate and serve with brandy butter.

- 75g dried mango
- 150g dates
- 150g dried figs (woody stems removed)
- 125g raisins
- 200g Demerara sugar
- 3 tbsp brandy or rum (or whisky or Armagnac)
- 2 oranges, juice and zest
- 75g fresh white breadcrumbs
- 75g plain flour
- 2 tsp mixed spice
- 50g almonds, finely chopped
- 100g butter, softened to room temperature, plus extra for the pudding bowl
- 2 large eggs, beaten

Prep: 30 mins
(plus 6 hrs for soaking)

Cook: 6–8 hrs

Serves: 8–10

Need a bit of help? Watch the video at www.abelandcole.co.uk/pudvid

Mulled Wine
. . . .

You know it's that time, when the mince pies are in the oven, and George Michael (then Bob Geldof, then Cliff Richard, then The Pogues) serenades you from the ghetto blaster. It's time to get a large saucepan out of the cupboard and get mulling.

Test the wine, a large glass should do the trick (although you'll need a full bottle of wine in the pan for the recipe to work). Put all the ingredients into a biggish pan. Gently simmer for 30 mins. Serve your mulled wine warm, preferably with a mini mince pie.

- 1 bottle of red wine
- 4 tbsp Demerara sugar
- 4 tbsp raisins
- 2 cinnamon sticks
- 3 clementines, sliced
- 6 cloves
- 50ml cognac (optional, but divine)
- 100ml water

Prep: 5 mins
Mulling: 30 mins
Serves: 6 (or 4, or 7... depends)

Mulled Apple Juice
. . . .

Simmer all your ingredients in a pan over a very low heat for 15–30 mins. If you do want this one alcoholic, add a splash or two of whiskey (or whisky, depending where your allegiances lie).

- 1 cinnamon stick
- 2 cm ginger root, peeled
- 2–3 tsp Demerara sugar
- 750ml–1 ltr apple juice
- 2–3 apple slices, studded with cloves

Prep: 2 mins
Mulling: 15–30 mins
Serves: 4–6

Christmas crackers

There is one day of the year when I can legitimately get away with telling lots of really awful jokes. This page is a tribute to that day.

Why does Santa have 3 gardens?
So he can ho-ho-ho.

What did Snowman A say to Snowman B?
'Can you smell carrots?'

Why did the baker get an electric shock?
He stood on a bun and a currant ran up his leg.

Why did the King go to the dentist?
To get his teeth crowned.

What's white and goes up?
A confused snowflake.

Which nut sounds like a sneeze?
A cashew nut.

Why did the scientist install a knocker on his door?
He wanted to win the no-bell prize.

What do snowmen eat for breakfast?
Snowflakes.

Darth Vader: Luke, I know what you're getting for Christmas.
Luke: How?
Vader: I can feel your presents.

Who hides in the bakery at Christmas?
The mince spy.

Spring

Blossom, foraging, daffodils, marathons, maypoles

Springing a leek

Spring

Spring starts with the Spring Equinox on 20th March. Spring ends on 20th or 21st June with the Summer Solstice.

Look out for

Purple sprouting broccoli in March

Asparagus in April

New potatoes in May

Rhubarb in June

Things to do in Spring

Go blossom spotting

Feed the ducks

Carry sunglasses and an umbrella about your person every day for three months

Dust off the barbie?

Tie some bells to your knees and eat raw asparagus for the first time

Sniff out some free wild garlic

When Spring became Summer (and Winter, and Autumn)

Ever get the feeling that someone's put all the seasons in a bag and shaken them up?

We used to be able to say for sure that June meant broad beans, but the weather is a little more erratic than it used to be. As I write this, some crops are running five weeks late. They think it's still Spring. It's the last week of July.

Thankfully our farmers are worth their salt. No matter what the weather throws at them, they always turn up with a tractor load of veg and a smile.

Spring is... asparagus

Fenland farmer Clive Martin grows asparagus for us each year (and rhubarb, and squash, and globe artichokes) on Bedlam - the name of his farm - which is at odds with his efficient, pristine set up.

Organic asparagus needs a lot of time and attention dedicated to it to make it thrive. It's the same for all organic crops.

Investing in things that matter and having a respectful relationship with suppliers is vital to any healthy business.

We are friends with our farmers and work in collaboration with them. In return we get interesting, beautiful food. We even give the odd interest-free loan (for new orchards, milking parlours, that kind of thing).

Show me a supermarket that has an email inbox full of its farmers' new kittens/babies/holiday snaps and I'll eat my mousemat.

Asparagus

Asparagus is the poster veg for seasonal eating. It's unique, wonderful and gorgeous, just like my wife Chippy.

It's only around for a few weeks as it needs to be left to grow back for future Spring harvests.

Asparagus tips
. . . .

Crunch bunch

Raw asparagus is really, really good. Slice it into little discs and dress with lemon juice, zest, olive oil and chilli.

Best secret toast tip

If you toast whole asparagus in a hot, dry frying pan (with no oil, butter or water) it goes amazingly nutty. You'll never steam again. Once it's picked up a little barbecuesque char, serve with a dot of butter, a squeeze of lemon and a sprinkle of salt.

♡ Asparagus loves...

Soft boiled duck eggs (big yolks are all the better for dunking with), mozzarella, chilli, orange, lemon, wild garlic, shellfish, new potatoes, salt, pepper, Parma ham.

Squeeze of the month

Warm a baking tray. In a bowl, coat trimmed asparagus with olive oil, lemon juice and a smidge of salt. Roast the asparagus and a quartered lemon till tender. Squeeze the roasted lemon wedges over before serving. Inhale.

Rasher decision

Wrap Parma ham, pancetta or a thin piece of bacon around each raw spear. Grill on high or roast till the bacon is cooked and the spears are crisp and tender. Perch on a mound of scrambled eggs.

Storage tips

Keep asparagus in the fridge or the spears will go all bendy. Nobody wants that. Save the woody ends for stock or risotto.

Beetroot

Heard of Royal Blue? What about Royal Pink? Sexagenarian skating champion, Monty Don lookalike and organic farmer, John Danby, grew this pretty stripy Chioggia beetroot for us last year. A few people took a particular liking to it, then Prince Charles presented him with a 'best veg' Soil Association award for it.

Super fast beets

Beetroot doesn't need to be boiled or roasted for hours. Just peel, slice into chunks and fry in a little olive oil. Clang on a lid, and cook for 10 mins. Once it's softened a little, season and serve as a side dish or add to salad.

Won't cook, don't cook

Beetroot is fantastic raw. Make a grated beetroot and carrot salad with toasted seeds and a honey and mustard dressing. Punchy.

Stunning salads

Chioggia and golden beetroot are more delicate than ruby red roots. So much so, they don't need cooking at all.

Let them shine in salads. Just thinly slice and layer with rocket, olives and any other salady bits you've got lying around.

Eaty leafy

You can eat beetroot leaves. Just rinse and use as you would chard or spinach. Or make them into pesto (see page 186).

♡ **Beetroot loves...**

Apple, feta, watercress,
pepper and olive oil,
carrots, chocolate,
Puy lentils.

Seriously Phenomenal Dark Chocolate Beetroot Cake

Beetroot lends a lovely moistness, a sweetness and a rich, ruby tinge to this cake. You won't taste a smidge of veg, so it's perfect for people who (think they) don't like beetroot.

Roast or boil your beetroot till tender (takes about an hour). Peel or cut off the skin. Roughly chop, then purée (this can be done in advance).

Preheat the oven to 180°C/Gas 4.

Pop the chocolate and beetroot in an ovenproof bowl. Put it in the warming oven just till the choc melts. It only takes a few mins, so check often.

Fold the melted choc and beetroot together. Mix in the ginger (and cardamom, if using). Set aside to cool.

Mix the flour, baking powder and salt in a large bowl.

Whisk the egg yolks with the butter and sugar till pale and creamy. Whisk the whites till stiff and meringue-like. Gently fold the yolk mix into the flour. Then fold in the whites, one spoon at a time.

Gently stir in the beet-choc mix. Grease an 18 cm (7") cake tin with butter. Dust with enough flour to coat. Pour in the mix. Bake for 50 mins or till a skewer comes out clean. It will be almost fudgy in the middle.

Stand for 10 mins. Turn out and cool on a rack. Mix all the icing ingredients together by stirring, or use a handmixer.

Ice your cake. Grate over the zest of an orange, if it takes your fancy.

- 200g ruby red beetroot (not golden or Chioggia)
- 150g dark chocolate, roughly chopped
- 1 tbsp freshly grated ginger
- ½ tsp ground cardamom (optional)
- 125g plain flour
- 1½ tsp baking powder
- A pinch of sea salt, finely crushed
- 3 eggs, separated
- 200g unsalted butter, at room temperature
- 150g caster sugar

For the mascarpone icing:
- 100g mascarpone cheese
- 200g cream cheese
- 75g icing sugar, sifted
- 1 tsp ginger, freshly grated
- 1 orange, zest (optional)

Prep: 20 mins
Cook: 1 hr 50 mins (includes beetroot cooking time)
Serves: 8 (well, it depends...)

How to HAKUNA FRITTATA

THE FRYIN' KING

VEGETARIAN
ANY VEG HAKUNA FRITTATA

In a bowl, whisk the eggs then fold in some cooked, but cooled, veg (see opposite for our suggestions). Season well and add chilli and/or herbs, if using.

Tip the egg-veg mix into a frying pan brushed with olive oil. Cook on a medium heat for a few mins. Scatter on some cheese and pop it under the grill.

Cook till golden on top (about 10 mins, depending on how deep the pan and egg-veg mix is).

It's worth finding out where your eggs come from. Organic eggs have a lovely rich flavour. Organic standards guarantee the hens have a truly free range life, a nutrient rich diet and no GM food.

- 6 eggs
- 1–2 mugs of seasonal veg, chopped and cooked (see opposite)
- ½ mug of spring onions, leeks or onions, finely chopped and sautéed in oil with garlic
- 1 mug of cheese, crumbled or grated (see opposite)
- A handful of fresh or dried herbs (if you have any)
- Some finely chopped chilli, or chilli powder (optional)
- Sea salt and freshly ground pepper

Prep: 10 mins

Cook: 25 mins

Serves: 4–6

PAC PAN

Throwing together a frittata makes veg go much further. So it's great for precious asparagus, purple sprouting broccoli and broad beans. Any veg'll do though, and if you have a scrap of cheese and some herbs, you're on to a winner.

FRITTATARING IT ALL AWAY

Deep greens

For the egg mixture: finely chop some kale or cavolo nero and a tin of salted anchovies, and sauté with the onions. Before you grill it: add parsley if you have any.

Spring greens

For the egg mixture: finely chop some greens and add them to the pan after you've softened your onions and garlic. Before you grill it: throw in crumbled goat's cheese, finely chopped red chilli and rosemary.

Purple sprouting greens

For the egg mixture: snip purple sprouting broccoli (heads, stalks and leaves) into bite-sized pieces and fry with some onions and garlic. Before you grill it: add blue cheese or strips of Parma ham.

Scarborough fayre

For the egg mixture: slice and sizzle mushrooms with some onions and garlic till golden. Add a glug of balsamic and cook till it's absorbed. Before you grill it: top with a heap of grated Parmesan and parsley, sage, rosemary and thyme.

Zesty greens

For the egg mixture: cook grated or sliced courgettes with some onions and garlic. Before you grill it: dust with lemon zest and grated cheddar.

Bunched carrots

If you're ever stuck talking to a rabbit at a party, don't start humming Bright Eyes, and for peat's sake don't mention Bugs Bunny. The rabbit community are still hopping mad. All that unauthorised product placement... will they sue for misrepresentation (they much prefer lettuce)?

Of course not. Because it's a cartoon, and rabbits aren't allowed in courthouses.

Storage tips

These are more delicate than main crop carrots. So store them in your fridge drawer and don't leave them for too long.

I've got a lovely bunch of carrots (tiddly pom)

Carrot tops

Bunched carrots are slightly sweeter than the main season crop and they're wonderful in the recipes on page 206.

It's the leafy green tops we're concerned with here. They're a bit coarse yet have a lovely carroty-parsley flavour.

Use them as a garnish (as you would parsley) in soups, stews and couscous.

If you're making stock, carrot tops add a rich flavour and golden hue. Plunge them in towards the end of cooking.

Yellow tip road

The Victorians used carrot leaves to dye things yellow and so can you.

Just boil them up with some vinegar. Use the yellow liquid to dye eggs (see page 138–139). Or experiment and use the dye for other craft projects.

Here the wild things are

Wild Garlic. Untamed, carefree, unbound by the trappings of farming social norms. Unaccustomed to combine harvesters and humans.

Kept company by bluebells, croci, and the odd squirrel. Until now.

How to spot wild garlic

Wild garlic, also known as ramsons, looks a bit like tulip leaves, just more delicate and herby.

It grows in Spring and is happiest in ancient woodland.

So go to the oldest bit of nearby heath/parkland/forest/countryside you know and weed out a semi-shaded spot with a natural water source nearby (wild garlic likes slightly moist conditions).

Put that conk to good use. It smells like spring onions and garlic.

Seek it then eat it

Wild garlic leaves are delicious in salads, or sprinkled on soup, swirled through mashed spuds and sneaked into sarnies.

They also make a fantastically garlicky pesto, see page 186.

Abide by the forager code

Leave enough for other foragers, other animals, and the land.

Happy sniffing and picking!

Chard

If you didn't know your greens, you'd think chard is a shape shifter. Charming as it is, it's not magical. There's just three types. Now you're here you'll know that the Italian stuff is wider and shorter. The UK stuff looks more like spinach. And rainbow chard has beautiful coloured stalks.

VEGETARIAN
Chilli Chard Rice with Buttered Cashews

Lightly toast your rice in a large lidded pan. Add a pinch of salt and a glug of olive oil. Stir.

Pour the water over the rice. Let it sizzle up. Cover. Reduce the heat. Cook for 10 mins.

In a different pan, fry the onion in a little oil with a pinch of salt. Once glossy and soft, add the garlic and chilli. Let them soften. Fold in the chard. Add a good squeeze of lemon and some salt and pepper.

Let the rice steam for 5 mins once the 10 min cooking time is up. When it's fluffy and all the water's gone, plonk it in a dish. Pile the veg on top. Gently mix.

Wipe your pan clean. Melt the butter. When it starts to froth, add the cashews and a pinch of salt. Fry over a lowish heat till golden. Scatter the nuts and their butter over the rice.

Finish with grated lemon zest and extra chilli, if you like.

- 1 mug of white basmati rice
- 2 mugs of water
- Sea salt and freshly ground pepper
- Olive oil
- 1 onion, thinly sliced
- 3 fat garlic cloves, finely chopped
- 1 small red chilli, finely chopped (to taste, remove seeds for less heat)
- 4–6 large handfuls of spinach or chard
- 1 lemon, juice and zest
- 2 tbsp butter
- 2 large handfuls of cashews

Prep: 10 mins
Cook: 20 mins
Serves: 4

Storage tips

For maximum shelf life, wash your leaves when you get them. Shake dry. Wrap in a clean, dry tea towel. Store in the fridge in a spot where they won't get crushed.

Know your Greens

Everyone knows that greens are good for us. What's not always clear is who's who.

Chard

These dark, thick leaves are fab in quiche, pasta or rice.

Chinese leaf

This fantastic Winter green looks like the love child of a savoy cabbage and an iceberg lettuce. Perfect in stir-fries, kimchi or P.T.O.

Pak choi

Lighter and blousier than chard, this is stunning raw in salad with a punchy lime, ginger and chilli dressing.

Spring greens

The most cabbagy of the lot. Blanch these greens (plunge in boiling water for two mins), then toss with butter and sea salt.

Chinese leaf

When our wild haired Welshman Nick Briggs isn't playing saxophone on the telly, he sources all our high welfare, free range meat and poultry. He's as good at buying sausages and inventing recipes as he is at playing music with famous people.

VEGAN
Chinese Leaf Parcels

When Nick makes this, he fries up some free range pork mince along with the mushrooms and onions.

Carefully pull off 8 large outer leaves of your Chinese leaf and finely shred the rest.

Rice first: pop a lidded pan over medium heat. Toast the rice for a mo. Add a pinch of salt and a drizzle of oil. Add the water. Stir. Let it bubble up. Cover. Reduce the heat. Cook for 30–40 mins, till the water is absorbed. Check occasionally. Add more water if needed.

In the meantime, fry your mushrooms and onions or leeks till golden and tender. Add the shredded Chinese leaf, garlic, ginger and chilli. Stir and cook till soft. Season with soy sauce, lime juice and zest. Taste and adjust accordingly. Add herbs, if using.

When both are cooked, stir the rice and veg together.

Now the parcel: put your leaves and a pinch of salt in a large dish or bowl. Pour enough boiling water over to just cover. Turn the leaves and remove when softened. It'll take a couple of mins.

Pat the leaves dry. Spoon a heap of the rice mix onto the firm white stalk of the leaves. Fold the leafy ribbed bit over. Tuck in the sides and you've got a divine parcel of yum.

*Brown rice is gorgeous in this (and better for you). If you're short of time, white rice only takes 12 mins to cook.

- 1 head of Chinese leaf
- ½ mug of brown rice*
- 1 mug of water
- Sea salt
- A few splashes of olive oil
- 200g mushrooms, thinly sliced
- 1 onion, 2 leeks or 4 spring onions, chopped or thinly sliced
- 2 garlic cloves
- 3 cm piece of ginger, peeled and finely grated
- ½ red chilli, finely chopped (to taste)
- A few splashes of soy sauce
- 1 lime, juice and zest
- A handful of fresh coriander leaves, to garnish (optional)

Prep: 15 mins
Cook: 40 mins
Makes: 8

Storage tips
Leaf it in the fridge.

Jersey royals & New potatoes

Is it a cardigan? Is it a jumper? Nope – it's a small, flaky potato. Jersey royal spuds herald the start of the potato season. Grown exclusively on the balmy hills of Jersey, they're only around for a handful of weeks each year.

Jersey royals have waxy yellow flesh and delicate skin that just needs washing, not peeling. Any new, waxy spuds will work in these ideas.

Tatty tips

Cardigan curry

Use gently boiled Jerseys as the main feature (instead of meat or fish) in a curry. Their sweet, nutty taste and texture make them a worthy alternative to meat.

Pestotatoes

Boil till tender, drain, then stir in some fresh pesto (make your own, page 186). Add some freshly chopped mint for a lift.

Royal salmon

Mix cooled, boiled Jersey royals with crème fraîche, a touch of lemon juice and zest and cold roast salmon flakes. Top with chervil or rocket.

Munch brunch

Quarter your spuds and boil till just tender. Drain and cool. Snip pancetta or streaky bacon into lardons and gently fry. Add the potatoes and a glug of olive oil or butter. Fry for a little bit. Delicious with a poached egg.

Nice was, niçoise

Boil and slice your spuds and mix with tinned tuna, black olives, boiled eggs and cherry tomatoes.

Tit for tzatziki

Mix cold boiled Jerseys with Greek yogurt, cucumber, lemon, garlic and mint (or a tub of tzatziki) for instant potato salad.

Hungry as a horse

Mix some horseradish sauce with crème fraîche and freshly chopped parsley. Stir through a bowl of cold, boiled potatoes.

Sea shanty spuds

Toss boiled Jerseys with white crab, a bit of melted butter, lemon juice and fresh red chilli (for a spicy shanty).

Patatas chorizo tortilla

Add some chunks of chorizo, finely chopped onion, parsley and sliced new spuds to a bowl of whisked eggs. Pour into an oiled pan. Grill or bake till set.

Ginger Rogers & Basil Fawlty

Qué? Gently fry boiled Jerseys with a bit of butter and freshly grated ginger. Season and garnish with fresh, torn basil leaves.

Storage tips

Keep them in a dark bag (brown paper bags do just fine – like the ones we deliver our potatoes in) in a cool, dry place. They're delicate, so use them reasonably quickly.

Leeks & Spring onions

When the weather's really grim, and it's June, pass the allium (not the Valium). They'll pick up any dish you introduce them to. They're interchangeable in recipes that call for them cooked. Leeks are the woodier, milder Winter version and spring onions are the punchier little guys that arrive just as leeks go out of season.

VEGAN
Sizzle & Spice Spring Leek Chickpeas

A gorgeous vegan main for 2, or a side dish for 4. Lovely with a warm naan.

In a large, hot frying pan, sizzle leeks or spring onions with a splash of oil till glossy and softened a bit.

Add the ginger and garlic. Fry till tender. Stir in the spices, then the chickpeas. Heat through. Zing in the citrus juice and zest. Taste. Season. Taste again.

To make it a bit looser and saucier, if you wish, add a few splashes of water. Bung in a load of fresh herbs and plate up.

> ♡ **These alliums love...**
> Goat's cheese, feta, blue cheese, cheddar (pretty much all cheese actually), egg, chilli, lentils, peas, crème fraîche, white wine, roast lamb, mint, coriander.

- A few splashes of olive oil
- 1 large or 2 small leeks, or 6–8 spring onions, thinly sliced
- 3 cm ginger, finely chopped or grated
- 2 garlic cloves, finely chopped
- 1 tsp cumin seeds or ground cumin
- 1 tsp ground coriander
- 1 tsp paprika
- A pinch of ground cinnamon
- A pinch of chilli powder
- 2 tins of chickpeas, drained
- 1 lemon or 2 limes, juice and zest
- Sea salt and freshly ground pepper
- A handful of fresh herbs

Prep: 10 mins
Cook: 15 mins
Serves: 2–4

Colour me natural

If artificial colours aren't your bag, delve into
a veg box and let nature turn things pink.
Or blue, yellow, orange, lavender...

Colour	Magic ingredient
Buttercup yellow	Turmeric
Brick orange	Brown onion skins
Lipstick pink	Beetroot
Soft lavender	Red cabbage
Milk chocolate brown	Black coffee
Electric blue	Red cabbage with bicarbonate of soda

A couple of Easters ago, Rachel got creative with her veg box and created some very natural dyes. She then dyed some duck eggs and her family had the prettiest breakfast in town.

Duck eggs work best as their shells are big and white. Boil them for 10 mins. Drain and cool.

How dye you do

For each dye you'll need one saucepan, 2 tbsp of cider or white wine vinegar and 500ml water.

Then, add the following ingredients, depending what colour you want to make.

Buttercup yellow – 2 heaped tbsp turmeric

Brick orange – 2 mugs of crushed brown onion skins

Lipstick pink – 1 large, coarsely grated beetroot

Soft lavender – 1 mug of finely chopped or grated red cabbage

Electric blue – 1 mug of finely chopped or grated red cabbage

Bring the pot (or pots) to the boil then simmer for 20 mins. Make sure the water doesn't reduce too much. Add more, if needed.

Once the dyes have simmered and the colours look rich, get a mug (or mugs, depending on how many dyes you're making).

If making electric blue, add 1 tsp of bicarbonate of soda to that mug.

For milk chocolate brown, let a mug of strong black coffee (instant or ground) cool, then pop a boiled egg into the mug.

Using a tea strainer or muslin, strain the dye into the mugs. Put a boiled egg in each mug. Let them soak for at least 30 mins. The longer they soak, the richer the colour will be.

Remove them with a slotted spoon and let them dry in an egg cup. Refrigerate for up to 3 days.

Peel and dip in a pinch of salt or roll in a mix of crushed cumin, coriander and paprika.

Purple sprouting broccoli

If you're not artificially extending the seasons by using chemicals or heated greenhouses, Spring is a time for planting crops, not harvesting them. Luckily though, purple sprouting broccoli (or PSB) is the Usain Bolt of the veg world. It arrives faster than everything else.

A bunch of ideas

Colour fix flash pan

To keep PSB's lush purple hue, griddle, grill or quickly stir-fry it. Steaming and boiling washes its colour away. Stir-fry friends include ginger, soy sauce, lime juice and cashews.

Eggs and sprouting soldiers

Grill a few stalks of PSB till just tender. March them straight into the sunshine yellow yolk of a soft boiled egg. Use duck eggs if possible as they're bigger. Or dunk grilled florets into a melty whole baked brie.

Sidewalk salad

Griddle your purple broccoli in a dry frying pan till toasty and just tender. Eat the tips, tender stalks (compost any woody bits) and leaves with fresh crab, herbs, chilli and a lemon vinaigrette.

Fish for complements

Melt some oil or butter with a couple of tinned anchovies, add a good grind of black pepper and a touch of lemon juice and zest. Coat grilled or roasted PSB in the sauce. Cap with a poached egg if you've got one.

Purple Pancetta Pasta

Purple sprouting broccoli loves pasta. For a veggie or vegan twist, double the amount of dressing and add a good handful of toasted pinenuts or almonds.

Cook the pasta according to packet instructions. Drain. Gloss with olive oil.

Crisp the pancetta in a frying pan. Add a little oil if needed. Add the broccoli and cook till just tender but still purple.

Whisk together the oil, lemon juice, chilli and seasoning to make the dressing.

Stir together the pasta, pancetta and broccoli. Drizzle with dressing. Mix. Taste. Season. Finish with a little freshly grated Parmesan, torn mozzarella or toasted almonds for extra fabness.

♡ Purple sprouting broccoli loves...

Anchovies, lemon, garlic, almonds, chilli, goat's cheese, olive oil, mozzarella, crab, tomatoes, quiche, chorizo, pancetta, salted peanuts.

- 300g pasta, any shape (we use penne)
- A glug of olive oil
- 100g pancetta or streaky bacon, snipped into lardons
- 4 mugs of purple sprouting broccoli, cut into 3 cm bits
- Sea salt and freshly ground pepper
- Freshly grated Parmesan, mozzarella or toasted almonds (optional)

For the dressing:
- 3 tbsp olive oil
- 1½ tbsp lemon juice
- ½ red chilli, deseeded and finely chopped

Prep: 10 mins
Cook: 15 mins
Serves: 4

Rhubarb

Rhubarb rocks the compote. And compote has a multitude of uses. It's great for unpredictable Spring weather when the mercury suddenly drops and the sunglasses go back in the drawer.

> ♡ **Rhubarb loves...**
> Vanilla, strawberries, pork, ginger, apple, chilli, mackerel, cream.

Compotements

Ruby sundae

Dollop warm compote over a few scoops of vanilla ice cream. For an added treat, sneak in a round of shortbread.

Fools rush in (don't blame them)

Layer cold rhubarb compote with vanilla yogurt or custard. Sprinkle on a crunch of granola or toasted oats and some crystalised ginger.

Saucy roast

Swap the vanilla for 1 tsp of freshly grated ginger in your compote and cut back on the sugar. Smashing with warm roast pork.

Old school crumble

Mix your compote with halved fresh strawberries. Make a crumble topping to scatter over the top and bake till golden. Delicious with custard.

Nice rice

Swirl warm or cold compote through a batch of rice pudding. Add a little fresh or crystallised ginger to cut through the sweetness.

> **Storage tips**
> Rhubarb can be frozen. Clean and dry your stalks, and cut into pieces. Place spaced out on a baking tray in your freezer. Once frozen, put in freezer bags and use from frozen as required. Uncut stalks will keep for a week in the fridge.

VEGAN

Rhubarb Compote

Slice your rhubarb into 2–3 cm bits. Pop in a pan. Add the sugar and vanilla. Drizzle in enough water to just dampen the mix. Bring to the boil then lower the heat. Simmer till the rhubarb is tender – it'll go from firm to mush quickly so keep an eye on it. It shouldn't take more than 10–15 mins.

Taste, add more sugar (or honey) if needed. Drain the juice but don't chuck it, it's a great cordial for sparkling water or wine.

Chill for 3–4 days or freeze.

- 1 bundle of rhubarb
- 3–4 tbsp caster or Demerara sugar
- ½ vanilla pod (optional)
- 3–4 tbsp water

Prep: 5 mins

Cook: 10–15 mins

Serves: 2–4

Respect your elders

Whilst the berries and the leaves of the elder tree are poisonous, elderflowers are edible and drinkable.

All you need is your foraging cap firmly on, some scissors or secateurs, a bag and a hedgerow.

Elderflowers flourish in disused areas so find a quiet lane or neglected spot. You need about 15 large flower heads to make two litres of cordial.

Elderflower cordial

Firstly, shake your blossoms to remove any errant bugs and the like. Place in a very large, heatproof bowl with the lemon slices.

Put the sugar and water in a large saucepan, over a low heat. Stir till the sugar is fully dissolved. Turn up the heat and bring to the boil. When it's syrupy, pour the liquid over the elderflowers and lemon.

Cover with a plate or tea towel. Put in a cool place to steep for about 24 hours.

Strain through a muslin-lined sieve into a jug. Pour into bottles (or use jam jars). Store in the fridge for up to a week. Or, pour into ice cube trays and freeze till ready to use.

If you're going on a picnic, pop frozen cordial ice cubes into a jug with water and let them melt as you travel to your picnic spot.

- 15 large elderflower blossom heads
- 3 unwaxed lemons, sliced
- 1½ ltrs of cold water
- 1kg caster sugar

Prep: 10 mins
Cook: 10 mins
(plus steeping)
Makes: about 2 ltrs

Summer

Deck chairs, sunhats, umbrellas, messy ice cream hands, long evenings

Fruity Salad

Summer

Summer starts with the Summer Solstice on 20th or 21st June.
Summer ends on 21st September with the Autumn Equinox.

Look out for

Broad beans in June

Strawberries in July

British tomatoes
in August

Sweetcorn
in September

Things to do in Summer

Get a hammock

Get a solar powered radio (for
cycling and picnics)

Paddle

Play cricket in the office (it's
possible, we've lived to tell the tale)

Learn to accept that Summer is
something that mostly happens in
other countries

Go to the seaside at least once, even
if it rains, and eat an ice cream

The tip of the iceberg lettuce

Not all fruit and veg are as considerate as the coconut, which comes in its own protective packaging.

If tomatoes came in a shell, like coconuts, think of all the packaging that could be saved.

(Although throwing a salad together would involve a lot more throwing.)

We've used boxes, not bags, since 1988. Overly packaged food is bad for the environment, and having a bin full of unnecessary packaging is such a bore.

Summer is... beans

Summertime is bean time. Eating them when they're in season is something to look forward to. Why fly them here at a time when the most exciting thing in season is mince pies and mulled wine?

We've never airfreighted food and we never will. Boats do just nicely when our fields are a bit bare or for essentials that we can't grow here (coffee, chocolate...).

Locally and naturally grown food, eaten in the right season, is the best thing since sliced and fried broad bean pods.

The only food that should fly is a pancake.

Aubergine

Botanically classified as a berry, aubergines are part of the nightshade family, along with potatoes and tomatoes. Their substantial, almost meaty quality makes these bruisers brilliant in veggie and vegan feasts.

Aubergenius ideas

Dippy whole roast

Crank your oven to 200°C/Gas 6. Roast the aubergine whole for an hour, turning once or twice. If it's not totally soft and squeezy (take care with bare hands) cook it a little longer. Slice the green hat off and blitz the whole thing in a blender with some ground cumin, paprika, chilli powder, lemon juice, olive oil and sea salt. Chill. Dip.

Halfwayside

For a fast route to heaven, halve your aubergine before roasting. Slice through the green top and straight down to the bottom, so you have two pear-shaped pieces. Carve criss crosses into the white flesh. Rub in garlic, sea salt and olive oil. Roast till tender. Top with a dollop of spiced yogurt and herbs.

Veggie burger secret

Whizz a whole roasted aubergine (minus green hat) up with tinned chickpeas (a 50/50 mix) and a handful of breadcrumbs for lush veggie burgers. Add balsamic vinegar, garlic, rosemary, chopped black olives and lemon juice for an Italian slant. Or whack in chilli, cumin, paprika, mint and toasted nuts or dried fruit for a Moroccan twist.

Aubergine sleeping bags

Slice your aubergine lengthways into thin slices. Season and fry in a little oil till golden. Once cool, lay a few herbs and some fresh slices of mozzarella or crumbled feta over them. Roll up from one end. Secure with a toothpick and pop in a lunchbox or picnic basket.

♡ **Aubergine loves...**

Red pepper, tomatoes, balsamic vinegar, lamb, chilli, garlic, ginger, cumin, prosciutto, soft cheese (ricotta, goat's cheese), walnuts, pinenuts.

Aubergine No Meat Meatballs

These beauties are meat-free but certainly look the part. They're definitely not just for vegans.

Place a large frying pan over medium heat. Sizzle the aubergine and onion in a bit of oil.

When they've picked up a little colour and are almost done, add the garlic, a squeeze of lemon juice and grate over a good bit of zest.

Tip it into a food processor with the olives, chilli, herbs, balsamic vinegar, breadcrumbs and pinenuts, if using. Whizz till everything comes together. Or chop everything up on a large chopping board and mix. Season.

Taste. Add more herbs or spice if needed. If it's a bit dry, add a splash of olive oil. If it's too wet, add more breadcrumbs. Shape into balls. (Two aubergines will make about a dozen rounded tablespoon-sized balls.)

Fry the balls in olive oil. When browned all over, serve with spaghetti and tomato sauce, or have them on their own.

- A few splashes of olive oil
- 2 aubergines, cut into small cubes
- 1 smallish onion, finely chopped
- 3 garlic cloves, finely chopped
- Sea salt and freshly ground pepper
- 1 lemon, juice and zest
- A handful of pitted black olives
- 1 red chilli, finely chopped (or a pinch of chilli powder)
- A large handful of fresh basil or 1 tbsp chopped rosemary leaves
- 1 tbsp balsamic vinegar
- 1 mug of breadcrumbs
- 4 tbsp pinenuts, toasted (optional)

Prep: 10 mins
Cook: 35 mins
Serves: 4

Delicious Aubergine Croutons

Cut an aubergine into 1 cm discs. Quarter each slice. Pour milk or water into a shallow dish. Dampen the aubergine pieces. Mix flour or polenta with salt, pepper and any spice you fancy. Place damp aubergine pieces in the flour, a few at a time, shake them to coat well.

Heat olive oil in a large frying pan (about 1 cm deep). Add the quarters in batches. When cooked through and golden on each side, drain in a colander or on a slice of bread. Serve over pasta, soup, salad or pack into houmous-filled pitta.

- 1 aubergine
- 1–2 mugs of milk or cool water
- 1–2 mugs of plain white flour or polenta
- Sea salt and freshly ground pepper
- Some spices - chilli powder and cinnamon are good
- Olive oil

Prep: 10 mins
Cook: 15 mins
Serves: 2–4

Avocado

Avocados are a bit of a wonder food. They're full of vitamins and essential fatty acids. Believed by some to be an aphrodisiac, their name comes from a Mexican word for a particular part of the male anatomy.

Light bulb moments

A very good morning

Sliced avocado on toast with olive oil, lemon juice and sea salt is probably one of the best ways to start the day.

Mexican dress

Mix a ripe avocado with the juice of 2 limes or 1 lemon, a whisper of garlic, fresh mint leaves, sea salt, a drop of olive oil and a trickle of water. It's a spectacular salad dressing for crispy leaves with thinly sliced spring onions and radishes.

Holy guacamole

Mush avocado with garlic, a touch of diced tomato, fresh coriander leaves, sea salt and lime. It's the reason tortilla chips were invented.

Grainy day

Avocado is a star in any salad, particularly grainy numbers as it seems to bring everything together. Mix diced avocado through a batch of bulgar wheat with toasted almonds, rocket and the Citrus Dress on page 178.

VEGAN OR VEGETARIAN
Avocado Chocolate Mousse

This may seem mad but it works. Nothing makes you feel more smug than eating avocado for pud.

Scoop the avocado flesh into a blender, blend all the ingredients together. Taste and add more cocoa, honey and water if needed. Chill and serve with ripe pears, cherries, or berries.

- 2 ripe avocados
- 3 tbsp unsweetened cocoa powder
- 3 tbsp honey or agave syrup
- 1 tbsp cold water
- A pinch of cinnamon or a touch of vanilla (optional)

Prep: 10 mins
Cook: nil
Serves: 2–4

> ♡ **Avocado loves...**
>
> Soy sauce, Parmesan, fish, lemon, lime, coriander, mint, sea salt, black pepper, chilli, chocolate, honey, sweetcorn, red pepper, tomatoes.

Beans

Beans, beans, beautiful beans. Pesticide-free British beans are very green. Even when they're purple.

Beans are a sure sign of Summer, so even if the weather isn't holding up its end of the bargain, pour a glass of crisp white wine and make something sunny.

Summer Beans with Crispy Garlic

Add a thin layer of oil to a hot frying pan. Sizzle the garlic with a pinch of salt. Garlic can burn quite quickly, so as soon as it's golden and crisp, remove. Set aside.

Using the same pan and oil, fry your prepped beans for a short while. (This stir-fry method is great for beautiful black or purple beans as a quick sizzle will soften them without washing out their colour.) Season as they cook.

Just as they start to soften, glug in some balsamic vinegar. Let it simmer and reduce to form a little dotty glaze over the beans.

Grate some lemon zest over. Add a squeeze of lemon juice. Gloss with a drop more oil.

Pile the beans into a dish and scatter on the crispy garlic.

- 1 good sized garlic clove per person, peeled and thinly sliced
- A good splash of olive oil
- Sea salt and freshly ground pepper
- 1 generous handful of beans per person, topped and tailed
- A good glug of balsamic vinegar
- 1 lemon, juice and zest

Prep: 5 mins
Cook: 10 mins
Serves: as many as you like

Hello old bean

Flat ones, long ones, poddy ones, stringy ones, green ones, not green ones...

With peas on the inside, and outsides that can go in your insides, beans are the ultimate eco veg because they come in their own green packaging.

French beans

The simplest of the bunch. To prepare just chop off the top stem tips and pop in the wok or steam till crisp and tender.

Runner beans

Remove the stringy bit by running a veg peeler down each side. Slice into bite-sized bits and steam or fry till just tender. Alternatively, slowly simmer in a chilli infused tomato sauce for a beautiful bean stew.

Flat beans

Slightly different to runners, flats are smooth (not hairy) and they cook a little faster. Delicious thinly sliced and tossed into a stir-fry with ginger, chilli, garlic, soy sauce and toasted sesame seeds.

Broad beans

The most British of beans are incredibly versatile. They're soft enough to whip into dips or pesto. You can even turn them into falafel or just have them on toast (page 175). Or P.T.O.

Borlotti beans

Slip out of their dotty pods and simmer (they need about 30 mins). Dress with olive oil or butter, sea salt and black pepper. Or make them the star of an Italian soup or stew.

Sugar snap peas

Sugar snaps look like garden peas but you can eat the whole thing. Like mangetout, but sweeter. Crunch them raw, or lightly cook. Don't try to shell them - the peas inside are dinky!

Broad beans

Broad beans have a cushy little life. Safe in their snuggly downy duvet covers, they grow up in the bucolic British countryside. They're living the rural dream.

VEGETARIAN
Broad Bean Fritters

Sorry compost, we get to eat the pods these days.

Heat oil in a large saucepan or pot.

Tear the broad bean pods along their seam. Cut off any stringy sides and remove the beans. Slice each pod half into 2–3 cm pieces. Cutting them on an angle looks smarter.

Put the flour in a large bowl with the salt, pepper and chilli.

Place the milk in a separate bowl. Dredge the trimmed pods through the flour. Dip in the milk. Dredge through the flour again.

Test the oil by frying one pod; if it sizzles and rises to the top, it's ready. Fry till golden. Let them cool slightly.

Tuck in, or give them another fry to make them extra crispy. Dust with salt and serve. Dip them in sweet chilli jam for a life altering experience.

For the actual beans

Cook in a little white wine and butter. Serve with basil and/or mint. Or make the pesto (page 186) or have them on toast (page 175).

A word in your shell-like

Baby beans, lightly boiled for 5 mins, can be eaten with the white skin on. Older beans need to cook a bit longer, then be peeled.

- 1 ltr sunflower oil
- 10–12 broad bean pods
- 2 mugs of flour
- 1 mug of milk
- ¼ tsp sea salt
- ¼ tsp black pepper
- ¼ tsp chilli powder (or any other punchy spice)
- Red chilli jam (optional)

Prep: 15 mins
Cook: 15 mins
Serves: 2–4

♡ **Broad beans love...**

Chorizo, salty hams, bacon, white wine, basil, mint, feta, pinenuts, ricotta, mascarpone, chilli, lemon, barbecued lamb.

Storage tips

Keep these podfathers in the fridge. If you want them really cold (i.e. frozen), shell and boil for a few secs, plunge into cold water, then freeze. Cook straight from frozen, or defrost for salads or dips.

Chilli peppers

Chillies are not chilly and that's why they're so attractive. They're pretty hot on veg boxes too. Bung some chilli in the pan with pretty much nearly any veg and you'll set the world on fire.

Hot tips

Curry favour

Chilli is one of the trinity of spices used as the foundation for a curry (the others are ginger and garlic). Finely chop all three and fry with an onion for the base of a tasty meal.

Just can't get enough

Chillies are addictive. Start by adding a little pinch and before long you'll be adding a lot. There are very few ingredients that chillies don't complement. (Ok, fine - custard, you're right.) It adds ooomph to salad dressing, peps up stir fries and seriously livens up root veg.

Winter chillies

Chillies are grown in Summer but there's a great way to keep them longer. Just halve them horizontally and dry. Or, finely chop and slowly roast till they dry out. They sweeten a little this way so you can make homemade chilli flakes.

Storage tips

Chillies go off faster if they're in plastic. Unwrap and pop them in a little dish in the fridge. If you're not using them fast enough, halve and freeze or air dry.

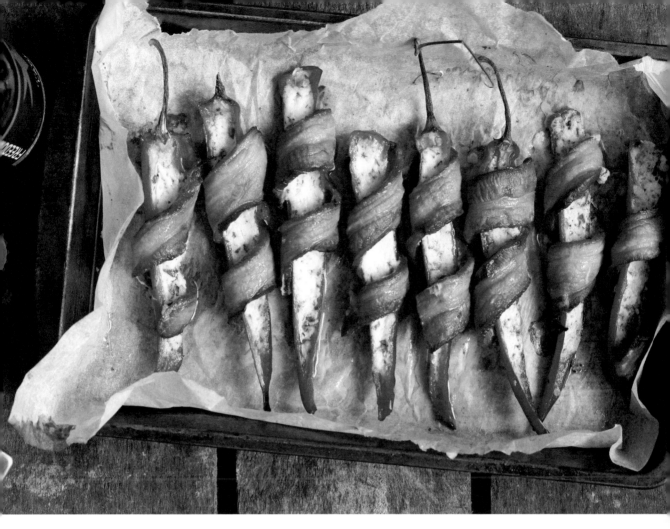

OMNIVOROUS
Chilli Peppers in a Blanket

These are the best post-pub snack in the universe. They're so easy and so good. They're also great with roast chicken, roast sweet potatoes and sweetcorn. Not a chilli fan? It works with ramiro peppers.

Preheat the oven to 200°C/Gas 6.

Halve the peppers horizontally, cut through the stem, keeping it intact. Scoop out seeds and membrane. Fold coriander through the cheese, if using. Fill the pepper halves with cheese.

Wrap each half in bacon, so it circumnavigates the pepper once. Fix with a cocktail stick or place in the baking tray so the bacon is secure.

Roast for 25 mins or till the bacon is done.

- 4–6 decent sized chilli peppers
- 200g cream cheese, fresh ewe's cheese or mascarpone
- 1 tbsp freshly chopped coriander leaves (optional)
- 8–12 rashers of smoked streaky bacon, long enough to wrap around the chilli halves

Prep: 15 mins
Cook: 25 mins
Serves: 4

Courgettes

Courgettes are a Summer squash (courge is French for squash). They can grow up to a metre long, although when that happens they technically become a marrow. If you can get your hands on the flowers, they're lovely stuffed with rice or cheese.

Gourd love 'em

Skinny dipping

Treat courgettes like cucumbers and cut them into batons and eat raw. Lovely dipped into a mustard vinaigrette or the Turkish Dress on page 178.

Cubism

Chop your courgettes into mini cubes. Throw them in a salad, or sizzle with other cubes of veg, onions, garlic and stock to make a quick bowl of soup.

VEGAN OR VEGETARIAN
Courgette Ribbons with Lemon, Chilli & Olives

Delicious as is, or stunning with fresh buffalo mozzarella, feta or fried halloumi (or fresh white crab meat).

Use a veg peeler to ribbon the courgettes lengthways. Work your way around the courgette as you 'peel' it right to the centre.

Drizzle a little olive oil over the ribbons. Grate on some lemon zest. Add the chilli, some lemon juice and olives. Give it a little taste.

Add a bit of honey or a pinch of sugar to mellow the tang of the olives and lemon. Season. Whack in a load of herbs. Taste again and fix seasoning as needed.

- 2 courgettes
- A good splash of olive oil
- 1 lemon, juice and zest
- 1 red chilli, finely chopped
- A handful of pitted black olives, roughly chopped
- A drop of honey or pinch of sugar
- Sea salt and lots of freshly ground pepper
- A handful of fresh mint and/ or basil, roughly chopped

Prep: 10 mins
Cook: nil
Serves: 4

Little Italian Courgette Cakes

Sneaking veg into cakes is almost a competitive sport at Abel & Cole. This recipe is one of our favourites.

Heat the oven to 180°C/Gas 4. Brush the inside of a twelve hole muffin tin with oil and dust with flour, or line with baking cups.

Whisk olive oil, sugar, eggs, lemon juice and zest, and cinnamon together till light and fluffy.

Sieve in flour, bicarb, baking powder and salt. Gently fold. Carefully swirl in the courgette, nuts and/or raisins. Save a few nuts for the tops. Don't overmix.

Divide the mix between the holes, just to the rim or a little below. Dot tops with nuts and/or raisins.

Bake for 25–30 mins, till a skewer comes out clean. Drizzle a little honey over the tops when you take them out of the oven.

The cakes will store for 2–3 days in an airtight container.

- 75ml olive oil
- 100g sugar
- 2 eggs
- 1 lemon, zest and 3 tbsp juice
- ½ tsp ground cinnamon
- 250g plain white flour
- 1 tsp bicarbonate of soda
- ¼ tsp baking powder
- A pinch of salt
- 1 mug of grated courgette
- A handful of crushed nuts and/or raisins
- A little honey

Prep: 10 mins
Cook: 30 mins
Makes: 9–12

Cucumber

Poet and songwriter John Gay first coined the phrase 'cool as a cucumber' in 1732, in his comic poem 'A New Song of New Similes' (thank you Tim Berners-Lee). Originally from India, cucumbers are technically a fruit and part of the squash family.

VEGAN

Quick Pickles

These quick pickles have that traditional sweet and sour tang but taste really fresh. Perfect for a barbecue.

Dissolve the sugar in the water. Stir in the vinegar then the courgettes or cucumbers. Season with salt, pepper and a good pinch of chopped herbs or spices. Mix well.

Spoon into jars (one or two should do). Don't worry if the liquid doesn't cover the veg. Refrigerate for at least 15 mins or up to 24 hours.

They start to go a bit soft after a day but I reckon you'll finish them before that.

- 2 tbsp sugar
- 1 tbsp boiling water
- 4 tbsp cider vinegar
- 1 mug of thinly sliced cucumber or courgettes
- Sea salt and freshly ground pepper
- Fresh herbs like mint, tarragon, dill – or try a pinch of coriander seeds and mustard seeds

Prep: 10 mins
Cook: nil
Serves: 2–4

♡ Cucumber loves...

Mustard, dill, ham, cheddar, feta, halloumi, oily fish, shellfish, mint, peanuts, strawberries, melon.

Fresh ideas

Tit for tzatziki

Grate or finely dice your cucumber and toss with sea salt. Mix natural or Greek yogurt with black pepper, finely minced garlic, lemon zest and olive oil. Fold in the salted cucumber. Add fresh mint, sorrel or dill. Delicious in a pitta with falafel or lamb.

Plato salad

Cucumber is essential in Greek salad. Cube and mix with diced tomatoes, sliced red onions, black olives, feta cheese, fresh oregano or thyme, a splash of red wine vinegar and olive oil. Mix the lot through a batch of tabouleh or couscous to make it more substantial. Feta accompli.

Globe artichoke

Whether you're sitting at the top of one playing a guitar, or eating them, I think we all agree that artichokes have a heart of gold.

Raiders of The Lost Artichoke

Trim the artichoke stalk, leaving just 3–4 cm, and make a criss cross cut in the end. This helps it cook faster.

Pour a couple of inches of water into a pot. Add the bay leaf and peppercorns. Pop a steamer basket or sieve on top. Add the artichokes. Cover.

Steam for 15–30 mins. The time depends on the girth of your artichoke. You'll know it's done when the base is tender, test it with the point of a knife.

Remove from the steamer. Let them cool while you whip up the garlic butter.

Melt the butter with the garlic and a pinch of salt. That's it.

Strip off the leaves and dip the meaty bits at the end of each leaf (the pale bit) in your garlic butter. Use your teeth to scrape it off.

Once you get to the centre, scrape out the fuzzy choke and discard. Quarter the heart. Dunk in butter and devour.

*Vegan option: use garlic, chilli and lemon infused olive oil instead of garlic butter.

See the video version of this at www.abelandcole.co.uk/recipes

- 2–4 globe artichokes
- 1 bay leaf
- 3 black peppercorns
- 1 garlic clove, finely chopped
- 50g butter*
- A pinch of sea salt

Prep: 5 mins
Cook: 25 mins
Serves: 2

Storage tips
As pretty as they look in a fruit bowl, these need to go in the fridge.

♡ Globe artichoke loves...
Parmesan, bay leaves, black pepper, butter, garlic, olives, cream, breadcrumbs, chilli, beetroot.

VEG BOX on TOAST

TOAST WITH THE MOST

You've heard of beans on toast. This is extreme beans on toast, and it may not even involve beans. Traditionally made, properly baked bread is naturally nutritious, so pile on some veg and have a proper meal. Sayonara spaghetti hoops.

Abel & Cole

Just about any veg is suitable as a topping on some old-fashioned toast.

TOP OF THE TOPPINGS

Beetroot, black pepper and brie.
Cook the beetroot first, and slice it.

Finely chopped broccoli florets and cheddar.
Use butter or olive oil as a spread. Add some tomato chutney if you're that way inclined.

Broad beans, fresh mint and feta.
Finish with a drizzle of olive oil.

Radish, sea salt and cream cheese.
Crunchy, salty and creamy.

Avocado, olive oil, lemon juice and sea salt.
Have this for breakfast and start the day on a high.

Kale pesto and goat's cheese.
See page 186 for our pesto recipe.

Whole roasted Portobello mushrooms and blue cheese.
Pop it under the grill for added oozyness.

Squished tomatoes, olive oil, fresh herbs and sea salt.
Perfect for any tomatoes that are a bit overripe.

Grated carrot, houmous, a drizzle of olive oil, black olives, fresh mint and basil.
You'll feel so virtuous you can probably skip the gym for a week.

Lettuce

A stunning Summer dress is nothing without...
a) a Keith on the arm, b) a matching handbag
or c) a fantastic lettuce.

Colin Andrews has been growing lettuce
(cos, romaine, lollo rosso, batavia, frisée,
oakleaf...) for us for years. He always says that
the odd hitch hiking bug means a healthy,
sustainable farm. A quick rinse, a delicious
dressing, and lunch is served.

Instant bagged lettuce

Bagged lettuce is convenient, but
this homemade version takes
seconds to prepare and is far more
environmentally friendly.

Trim the bottom of your lettuce. Separate
the leaves and rinse well (use a colander
if you have one).

Shake off the excess water. Dry in a salad
spinner or lay the leaves out on a clean
tea towel and pat dry. If they're still
damp, put them in the centre of a tea
towel, gather up the edges (so it makes
a parcel) and shake.

Line a bowl or plastic box with a clean,
dry cloth. This absorbs any excess
moisture. Put the leaves on the cloth
and cover with a tea towel or a lid.

Et voila. Bagged (or boxed) salad, washed
and ready to eat.

Super salad ideas

All you need is a bit of protein to turn a
bowl of leaves into a meal. Contenders
for this include: a punchy blue cheese,
toasted almonds, shredded leftover roast
chicken, a poached egg, or push the boat
out and treat yourself to some flaky roast
smoked salmon.

Vegetables that love leaves include grated
carrots or beetroot, courgette ribbons
(use that veg peeler), or cold boiled new
potatoes (which will help sponge up your
stunning Summer dressing).

VEGETARIAN
Turkish Dress
· · · · · · · · · · · · · · · ·

Gorgeous with dippable veg: red peppers, crisp lettuce leaves, radishes and cucumber. Or mixed leaves with herbs and crunchy croutons.

Mix together most of the yogurt, garlic, salt and pepper. Put the olive oil in a separate dish and swirl in a spoonful of yogurt. The mix will look a little curdled. Slowly incorporate this into the main yogurt mix till glossy and mayo-like. Add the herbs. Taste. Adjust seasoning. Keeps for 3–4 days in the fridge.

- 200ml natural yogurt
- ½ smallish garlic clove, minced
- Sea salt and freshly ground pepper
- 2 tbsp olive oil
- A few pinches of fresh herbs, finely chopped

Prep: 5 mins
Cook: nil
Serves: 4

VEGAN
Citrus Dress
· · · · · · · · · · · · · · · ·

Lovely on a grated carrot and beetroot salad, or with rocket or watercress.

Pour the olive oil and juice into a lidded jar. Add a pinch of salt. Shake, shake, shake. It should become a bit thick and creamy. Taste. Add a touch more juice if it takes your fancy. Shake again. Serve. Keeps for a week.

- 4 tbsp olive oil
- 4 tbsp orange or lemon juice
- A pinch of sea salt

Prep: 5 mins
Cook: nil
Serves: 4

VEGAN OR VEGETARIAN
Japanese Dress
· · · · · · · · · · · · · · · ·

Wonderful with courgette ribbons or grated courgette. Great with raw or griddled asparagus. Devilishly handsome with Winter roots, like roasted beetroot.

Pop everything into a jam jar or a cup. Shake or stir. Make sure you put the lid on if you're attempting the former. Taste, and add a little bit more of any of the ingredients, depending on how much you like them. Drizzle over your favourite hot or cold veg. Keeps for a week or two.

- 2 tbsp soy sauce
- 2 tbsp cider vinegar
- 1 lime, juice and zest
- 1 tbsp agave syrup or honey
- ½ garlic clove, finely chopped
- ¼ tsp fresh chilli, finely chopped
- ¼ tsp fresh ginger, finely grated

Prep: 5 mins
Cook: nil
Serves: 4

Crispy Duck Parcels
. . . .

Lettuce is a fantastic carb replacement. Treat it like a wrap and you can pile all sorts into it.

Leaves are far easier to find than rice pancakes. Their refreshing crunch is a brilliant contrast to the rich duck.

Heat the oven to 160°C/Gas 3.

Pop the duck legs in a roasting dish. Rub the chilli, ginger, garlic, soy sauce and honey into the duck.

Roast for 45 mins. Then crank the oven up to 220°C/ Gas 7 to help crisp the skin. Cook for 15 mins, or till the duck is crisp, golden and cooked through – test by piercing a fat part of the leg – if the juices run clear, it's done. Rest for 30 mins.

Slice onions and cucumber into wispy wands.

Shred the cooled duck. Stir some sauce through it.

Pile a mound of saucy duck onto a leaf. Top with cucumber and spring onion. Add extra sauce, coriander and lime juice, if you like.

*Vegan option: swap the duck for brown rice noodles and honey for agave syrup. Gloss warm, cooked noodles with some hoisin sauce. Pile into leaves with the other ingredients, as above.

- 2 duck legs*
- A red chilli, chopped
- A thumb of fresh ginger, chopped or grated
- 2 garlic cloves, chopped
- A splash of soy sauce
- A drizzle of honey*
- 4–5 spring onions
- ½ cucumber
- Some big lettuce leaves, washed
- A jar of hoisin sauce
- Fresh coriander leaves (optional)
- 1 lime, juice (optional)

Prep: 15 mins

Cook: 1 hr

Serves: 2–4

Tomatoes

If you're like my family and I, having tomatoes all year round is pretty handy. They're at their best in the Summer though. Of course, the absolute best tomatoes are eaten straight from your veg patch on a hot British August day.

VEGAN

A Really Good Tomato Salad
....

This is a dazzling little salad with a Moroccan feel. Offer it up as a tapasy starter, or serve it with roast lamb, halloumi, fish or lentils.

Halve or slice your toms. Season. Add the garlic and spices. Mix well so the tomato juice makes a dressing.

Add a glug of olive oil. Fold in the herbs. That's it. Refrigerate for up to a day, but bring to room temp before serving.

Have a crusty piece of bread to hand for mopping.

- A punnet of ripe tomatoes (any size will do)
- ½ garlic clove, finely chopped
- Sea salt and freshly ground pepper
- A pinch of ground cumin
- A speckle of chilli powder
- A glug of olive oil
- A small handful of fresh mint
- A small handful of fresh coriander

Prep: 5 mins
Cook: nil
Serves: 4

Storage tips

It's best to store your tomatoes at room temperature, at least for a day or two till they ripen. They need to go in the fridge if they arrive ripe, or when it's warm; warm Spring or Summer days, or simply a warm house. Bring them out of the fridge for an hour or two before eating.

Life in the freezer

If you have a glut, just pop tomatoes in a plastic container and freeze them whole. Use in stews and sauces from frozen.

Cool Tomato Soup with a Tickle of Moroccan Spice

Grab some tomatoes and an onion from your veg box, some spices from your cupboard and a piece of stale bread. Almost as quickly as you can say Hugh Fearnley-Whittingstall you'll have the most gorgeous organic soup.

Cook the onion and spices in some oil over moderate heat. When the onions have softened, add the tomatoes, breadcrumbs and honey. Stir and heat through.

Tip it all into a blender with lime juice, herbs and a little lime zest. Blitz till smooth. Taste. Season if needed. Press it through a sieve for a smooth soup, or leave it chunky.

Pop the soup in the freezer for 15 mins to eat chilled, or warm it in the pot to have it hot. Serve with a smattering of herbs.

- 1 onion, finely chopped
- A splash of olive oil
- 1 tsp paprika
- ¼ tsp ground ginger
- ¼ tsp ground cumin
- A good pinch of ground cinnamon
- 4 mugs of tomatoes, diced
- 1 slice of stale bread, crumbled
- 2 tsp honey
- 1 lime, juice and zest
- Sea salt and freshly ground pepper
- A handful of fresh coriander and/or mint, plus extra to garnish

Prep: 5 mins
Cook: 20 mins
Chill: 15 mins (optional)
Serves: 2–4

Honey Roast Tomatoes

Roast tomatoes are sweet and these bee-kissed babies are so easy. Perfect squished on to a piece of lightly toasted bread, or as a tomato base for pizza.

Preheat the oven to 200°C/Gas 6.

Grab a good handful of tomatoes and put them in a roasting tray. Drizzle the olive oil and honey over them. Throw a few herby sprigs in the mix. Sprinkle with salt and roast for 30–40 mins, till the tomatoes look soft, sweet and ready to squash.

- A few handfuls of tomatoes
- A glug of olive oil
- A drizzle of honey or agave syrup
- A few sprigs of rosemary or thyme
- A good sprinkle of sea salt

Prep: 5 mins
Cook: 30–40 mins
Serves: 2–4

My other JAR'S a VEG BOX

Thought pesto just came in jars? Think again. Pesto comes in veg boxes.

You can use all sorts of veggies and leaves. You can also make pesto with nettles, indeed. Just be sure to wear gloves when you pick them.

BESTO PESTO

MY OTHER TRACTOR'S A VEG BOX

Abel & Cole

EXPERIMENTAL PESTO

Tumble nuts or seeds, Parmesan, veg and chilli (if using) into a food processor. Add a glug of olive oil.

Blitz till you have a nice paste. Make it as smooth as you wish, adding more oil as needed.

Taste. Add more nuts or seeds, seasoning, Parmesan, veg or chilli as needed.

Serve immediately. Or pop into a jar, drizzle a bit of oil over the top, cover and store in the fridge for 3–4 days. It freezes well.

Use in pasta, toast, sandwiches, with potatoes (page 134), swirled through mash, pizza topping (page 82), as a dip. Thin with lemon juice, oil or natural yogurt to make a salad dressing, use to dress warm butter beans, warm with cream or butter to make a sauce for fish and so much more.

- ½ mug of seeds or nuts (pinenuts, almonds, walnuts, sunflower seeds...), toasted
- 1 mug of freshly grated Parmesan
- 4 handfuls of one of the below veg
- Fresh red chilli (to taste), chopped
- A glug of olive oil
- A pinch of sea salt

Prep: 10 mins
Cook: a couple of mins to toast the nuts
Serves: 3–4

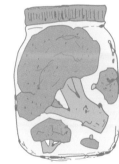

TRIED AND TESTED FAVOURITE THINGS TO PESTO

Purple sprouting broccoli or normal broccoli florets.

Radish leaves (sorry compost bin).

Raw broad beans (podded and peeled).

Spinach.

Cavolo nero (cut any tough stems off).

Kale (woody stems removed).

Brilliant Broccoli Pesto

Whizz up some raw broccoli with toasted walnuts and cubes of feta. Add a little olive oil and seasoning, depending on how you feel, and how it tastes. It's really good mixed with cooked bulgar wheat.

Radish

The crunchy, peppery bite of a red or black radish will liven up all sorts of stir-fries and salads. If you've got a black radish, you'll want to peel it first.

VEGAN
Radish Salsa
• • • • • • • • • • • • • •

Paul our lunch club chef makes this for us when we've been good little girls and boys. He's awesome and this is fantastic.

Mix everything together. If you wish, chop it all up in a food processor. Taste. Adjust seasoning.

Have it in pitta with smoked mackerel pâté. Or piled next to fresh grilled mackerel. Or with crisp lettuce and houmous. Or tossed with cool rice noodles with a dash of soy sauce and sesame oil.

• 1 bunch of radishes, finely diced
• ½ red onion or 1 shallot, finely diced
• 1 lemon, juice only
• A drop of olive oil
• 2 tsp balsamic vinegar
• A pinch of sea salt
• A handful of freshly chopped parsley

Prep: 15 mins
Cook: nil
Serves: 1–2

Inspiradish
• • • • • • • • • • • • • • •

Rawsome

Radishes are brilliant raw, so snack on them like grapes or pop them in a salad (sliced or halved).

Untradishional

For something quirkier than cucumbers, try thinly sliced radishes in a salted butter sandwich.

A leaf from our book

You can eat the leaves, too. Wash and use in a salad, or turn back a page and make pesto.

> ♡ **Radishes love...**
> Goat's cheese, hazelnuts, lime, mint, houmous, olives, mackerel, sea bass, hake.

Storage tips

Radishes can shrivel quickly at
room temperature so tuck them
into the fridge asap. Also, remove
the rubber band from the leaves
and they'll keep longer.

Rocket

It won't fly you to the moon, but these peppery leaves can catapult a salad to stardom.

Fast ways to fly

Seaside space mission

Our Christmas superstar Fiona Chalmers says a handful of rocket added to a tangle of pasta with crab, halved cherry toms, chilli and lime is divine.

Extraterrestrial

Add rocket, goat's cheese and a bowl of seasoned, whisked eggs to a warm pan glossed with olive oil. Pop it under the grill for a frittata (see page 122) or slowly scramble and heap on a slab of toast. Or go quiche. Out of this world.

Zoom to Italy

Adding rocket to a creamy risotto right at the end gently wilts the leaves and gives the risotto a dreamy texture and flavour contrast.

Venus di Milo

These leaves are a work of art, so let them shine in their purest form. Just spritz with lemon juice, a little zest, a gloss of olive oil and a pinch of sea salt. A masterpiece.

Storage tips

Shake your leaves into a bowl. Spritz with water; if you can, use a spray bottle. Tumble onto a clean tea towel. Pull the edges up to make a parcel of sorts. Shake the water off. Pop into a plastic tub lined with a fresh clean, dry cloth and they should stay perky and ready to eat for a week.

♡ Rocket loves...

Goat's cheese, lemon, crab, chilli, balsamic vinegar, cream, egg, tomatoes.

Watercress

In the Victorian era it was fashionable to walk around munching a bouquet of watercress. Reviving the old trend would certainly keep us vibrant. Our watercress farmer is in his eighties yet he leaps around like an energetic school boy.

A bouquet of ideas

Watercress dress

Add these to your leaves and they'll sing like Lulu. Balsamic vinegar, olive oil, lemon juice and zest. A pinch of sea salt, some grated beetroot and toasted pinenuts make it chart topping.

Ladle and bowl

Watercress soup is a classic for good reason. Sauté a finely diced onion till tender. Add small potato cubes and stock. Once mashably soft, add a big bunch of watercress. Blitz. Season to taste. Swirl in crème fraîche, a squeeze of lemon and some zest.

Witchy watercress

Think cucumber sandwich but with watercress. Simple and wickedly delicious. Slather two slices of sourdough (or a similar bread) with salted butter. Pile high with watercress. Add a squeeze of lemon. Sandwich and rejoice.

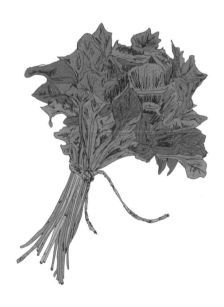

Storage tips

Watercress will keep longer if kept unbunched and away from plastic. Rinse and dry the leaves. Pop into a tea towel-lined plastic container and store in the fridge.

Sweetcorn

Badgers love sweetcorn. And so do we. Every year we lose a few ears (of sweetcorn) to the badgers, so our farmers set a little aside for them.

Sweetcorn is a seasonal treat and it's best when it's as fresh as possible.

Cornycopia

Grill it

Sweetcorn is ace on the barbie. Gloss the cobs with oil and a little salt. Grill till tender and just blistered. Brush with a spiced butter made by whipping half a mug of softened butter with spices (a good pinch of chilli powder, ¼ tsp ground cumin, ¼ tsp ground coriander, ¼ tsp paprika and ¼ tsp sea salt).

Roast it

If you don't have a barbecue, or if it's raining, heat the oven to 200°C/Gas 6. Heat a baking tray. Brush cobs with oil or butter, season and roast till tender.

Boil it

Get a pot of water rapidly boiling. Add a good pinch of salt. Plunge the cobs in and cook till just tender (5 mins).

Husky

Once you've stripped your cobs, keep the lovely husks. Use them to wrap nuggets of marinated meat or spice coated fish before roasting or putting on the barbie. Lay a few overlapping husks flat, then add meat or fish. Drizzle over a squeeze of citrus juice and olive oil, wrap and cook.

♡ **Sweetcorn loves...**

Butter, bacon, chilli, tomato, feta, quinoa, paprika, tuna, squash.

Sweetcorn & Cheddar Scones

These gorgeously moreish savoury scones are excellent for afternoon tea, lunchboxes, or with soup instead of bread.

Cut the kernels off the cobs, place in a pan. Add enough water to just cover. Simmer for 5 mins. Drain.

Heat your oven to 200°C/Gas 6. Mix the flour, baking powder, chilli and salt. Rub the butter cubes into the mix till it looks like fine crumbs.

Add the grated cheddar and corn. Drizzle in the milk. Gently fold to make a slightly sticky dough. Don't over mix.

Knead on a floured surface till just smooth. Divide into about 10 balls. Shape each roughly with floured hands. Place on an oiled baking sheet and brush the scones with a little milk.

Scatter grated cheese over the top. Bake for 10–15 mins or till the scones have risen, are golden and sound hollow when tapped on the bottom.

- 2 sweetcorn cobs, husked
- 350g self-raising flour
- 1 tsp baking powder
- A large pinch of chilli powder, to taste
- 1 tsp sea salt
- 50g cold butter, cut into cubes
- 150g grated cheddar, plus extra for tops
- 175ml milk, plus extra for brushing

Prep: 20 mins
Cook: 20 mins
Makes: about 9–12

Melon

Thankfully climate change hasn't quite got to the point where we can grow melons in Lincolnshire. Yet. So it's kudos to our Spanish farmers for sending us fragrant fruity balls from time to time.

Melon & Halloumi Salad

Oh hello. This impressive salad is fab at a barbecue. It works well as a large, help-yourself salad, or as a simple but smart starter.

Slice the melon into wedges. Carve off the skin.

Warm a large frying pan. Cut the halloumi into fairly thin slices. Crush the garlic with the side of a large knife.

Drizzle a thin layer of oil into the pan. Add the crushed garlic and halloumi. Fry till golden on each side. Keep an eye on the garlic – remove once golden and soft.

Pile a mound of rocket onto a large plate. Mix most of the herbs through, saving a few for the top. Lightly dress with citrus juice and zest, salt, pepper and olive oil. Mix well.

Layer the melon and halloumi into the salad. Finish with an extra drizzle of oil, a spritz of juice, a dot of sea salt and a final dash of herbs.

- ½ ripe melon, any variety (cantaloupe, honeydew, watermelon...)
- 150–200g halloumi cheese
- 4 small garlic cloves
- A few drizzles of olive oil
- A large handful of rocket or similar leaves
- A handful of fresh mint and/or basil
- 1 lemon or 2 limes, juice and zest
- Sea salt and freshly ground pepper

Prep: 10 mins
Cook: 10 mins
Serves: 2–4

> ### Storage tips
> Melons are fine at room temperature, but refrigerate once cut. To tell if it's ripe, smell the stem area on the top. If it's fragrant, it's ready to eat.

♡ Melon loves...

Cheese (feta, blue cheese, halloumi, goat's), pepper, mint, basil, rocket, lime, strawberries, sea salt.

Summer fruit

From the soft fruit and berries (strawberries, blueberries, raspberries, currants, gooseberries), to the stone fruit (apricots, peaches, nectarines and cherries), Summer fruits are nature's fruit pastilles.

Plucked from a punnet and straight in the mouth is the order of the day. However, if you have a glut, or prefer them cooked, read on.

OMNIVOROUS
Fruity Summer Garden Salad
....

Hull and halve your strawberries, or stone and slice your stone fruits. Toast the almonds in a dry frying pan.

Dress leaves with a pinch of salt, pepper, a splash of balsamic vinegar and a drizzle of olive oil. Add lemon juice. Toss. Arrange on plates or in a large salad bowl.

Tear the prosciutto or Parma ham and fold it into the salad. Scatter the cheese and fruit over the leaves and ham.

Drizzle a bit more olive oil and balsamic over the top. Finish with a scattering of toasted almonds, herbs and lemon zest.

- A few handfuls of strawberries, cherries, peaches, apricots or nectarines
- ½ mug of almonds, roughly chopped
- A few large handfuls of baby salad leaves
- Sea salt and freshly ground pepper
- A splash of balsamic vinegar
- A drizzle of olive oil
- 1 lemon, juice and zest
- 2–4 slices prosciutto or Parma ham
- 100g goat's cheese, crumbled
- A large handful of fresh mint, tarragon, chives and/or basil

Prep: 20 mins
Cook: nil
Serves: 2–4

Fruit machine jackpot

Blueberries

Best raw or warmed with sugar and a drop of water to make blueberry sauce for ice cream.

Raspberries

Pretty in fruit salad, with nectarines and edible flowers like nasturtiums.

Strawberries

Halve and mix with a pinch of sugar and some vanilla beans or essence. Layer in a glass with a mix of mascarpone and natural yogurt. Foolishly good.

Gooseberries

Cook with a little sugar, water and elderflower cordial till they burst into a tangy sauce. Serve with roast pork.

Currants (red, black and white)

De-stalk by holding the top of the stalk in one hand and run a fork down the vine with the other hand, over a bowl. Currants are tart, so use them in baking.

Nectarines

Wait till they give a little when squeezed and eat raw or slice into salad with goat's cheese and toasted almonds.

Peaches

Whether they are plump and round or flat and doughnut shaped, peaches are lovely raw. Or whipped into jam (for scones with cinnamon dusted clotted cream).

Apricots

Halve, stone and toss with a little sugar, vanilla and brandy. Roast and serve with toffee ice cream.

Gingery Roast Stone Fruit

If your stone fruit are a touch firm, or you just fancy something different, try this.

Crank your oven to 180°C/Gas 4.

Halve and stone your fruit. Place in a baking dish. Dust with Demerara sugar and freshly grated ginger.

Roast for 30 mins, or till the fruit is still holding its shape but is very tender and starting to caramelise. Amazing with toasted almonds and a dollop of yogurt or clotted cream.

- 4 peaches or nectarines, or 6 apricots
- 2–3 tbsp Demerara sugar
- 2 tsp ginger, freshly grated

Prep: 10 mins
Cook: 30 mins
Serves: 4

Summer Fruit Muffin Loaf

This used to be a muffin recipe, then we turned it into a loaf. You can turn any muffin recipe into a loaf by simply lengthening the cooking time (and using a loaf tin).

Heat your oven to 180°C/Gas 4. Oil a medium-sized loaf tin and dust with flour to stop the loaf from sticking.

Melt the butter; set aside to cool a little.

Mix the flour, baking powder, salt and sugar in a bowl.

Whisk the egg, milk and butter together. Fold through the flour mixture. Be careful not to overmix.

Swirl in the fruit and chocolate, saving a bit for the top. Pour the mix into the tin. Scatter the remaining fruit and chocolate over the top.

Bake for 45 mins, till golden and a wooden skewer inserted in the middle comes out clean.

- 50g unsalted butter
- 175g plain white flour
- 2 tsp baking powder
- ½ tsp salt
- 100g caster sugar
- 1 egg
- 120ml milk
- 125g Summer fruit (whole currants, pitted cherries, blueberries, raspberries or finely chopped strawberries)
- 100g white chocolate, chopped

Prep: 15 mins
Cook: 45 mins
Serves: 6–8

Storage tips

Berries and currants need to dash to the fridge asap. Let them warm to room temp 30 mins before serving. Unripe stone fruit is fine at room temp, in a cool place, away from direct sunlight. Keep an eye on them though and refrigerate when ripe.

Autumn

Winter

The fifth season

Lots of fruit and veg crop up in more than one season. And some of them are around for all four.

So we've used a little creative licence and made a fifth, omnipotent season.

Summer

Spring

A season for everything and everything in its season. Apart from the things in this chapter.

If Vivaldi had composed a cookbook, I reckon he might just have sneaked in a fifth movement.

The veg

New season carrots start in Spring and the main crop is harvested throughout Summer, Autumn and Winter.

The potato season starts in Spring with Jersey royals, moves on to new season spuds for the start of Summer and the main crop is harvested in Summer, Autumn and Winter.

And the fruit

Our relatively mild climate restricts us from naturally growing fruit all year round. It's great for berries (for a handful of weeks, at least) but not bananas. It's perfect for apples, but not pineapples.

So to eat fruit all year round, and get a bit of variety in our diet, we work with sustainable farmers further afield. It means we have more than just apples to choose from in December, and in Spring, when there's no British fruit to harvest, we have something sweet to snack on.

Broccoli

Ah broccoli. Thousands of little green flowers bursting with vits and flavour. Part of the brassica family, broccoli rhymes with Monopoly so pass Go, collect £200 and move three squares to the hob.

Floret fixes

Buttery

Broccoli's nuts about butter. Try this: sizzle a thick slice of butter till it froths up, turns a nutty golden brown and smells toffee-ish. Pour over steamed broccoli, or use as a broccoli dip.

Wedgie

To stop some bits cooking faster than others, quarter your head (of broccoli) into chunky wedges, then roast or steam. No steamer? Just cook your greenery in a shallow pool of water and cover. Cook till bright green and just tender. Add more water, if needed.

Pulsey

Cook some Puy lentils till soft (but not falling apart). Cut your broccoli florets into reasonably small pieces and steam. Let them all cool, then mix in a salad bowl with crumbled goat's cheese, a balsamic dressing and some fresh herbs.

> **Storage tips**
> Stand your broccoli in a small glass of water (in the fridge) to keep it perkier for longer.

> ♡ **Broccoli loves...**
> Cheese (Parmesan, blue cheese, mascarpone, goat's cheese), egg (great in quiche), almonds, garlic, cream, soy sauce, chilli, ginger, star anise (stir-fry), beans, pulses.

VEGETARIAN
Broccoli, Walnut & Feta Soup

Pop a large pot on medium heat. Add a splash of oil, followed by the onion, garlic and a pinch of salt and pepper. Cook till softened.

Stir in the potato cubes, pour in half the stock and simmer till tender.

Add half of the remaining stock and the broccoli. Cook for 3–4 mins so it's just tender yet still bright green.

Using a food processor or wand, whizz up the broccoli with half the feta and nuts. When smooth, taste. Add a bit more seasoning, broccoli or feta if needed. Add some parsley to intensify the colour.

Drizzle in more stock if the soup is too thick. Blend. Add a squeeze of lemon. Serve with the rest of the feta and walnuts scattered on top.

Make pesto, not soup? See page 186 for how.

- A glug of olive oil
- 1 large onion, finely chopped
- 2 garlic cloves, finely chopped
- Sea salt and freshly ground pepper
- 1 large potato, peeled and cubed
- 1 ltr veg (or chicken) stock, warmed
- 1 large or 2 small heads of broccoli, chopped
- 200g feta cheese
- A handful of walnuts, toasted
- A large handful of parsley (optional)
- A squeeze of lemon (if you have one)

Prep: 10 mins
Cook: 15 mins
Serves: 2–4

Carrots

Carrots were purple before William of Orange popularised the orange variety in the 1500's (my kind of marketing campaign). Bit more interesting than a business card, but it might make your wallet furry after a few weeks.

Carrot creations

Do the mashed carrot

Mashed carrots are delicious. Just peel, dice and simmer till tender. Mash them on their own, or with other mashable roots. Give them a twist by adding coconut milk, a little chilli powder and lime instead of butter. Garlic parsley butter is always a winner.

Roast sweet roast

Carrots sweeten when roasted. You can roast whole new season carrots (the slender ones with leafy tops). Halve or quarter larger carrots. Toss in olive oil, sea salt and pepper and roast at 200°C/Gas 6 till they're soft and starting to pick up a little colour.

Once roasted, mix with herbs and spices and eat as a side or stir into a bowl of freshly made couscous (or bulgar wheat, or quinoa, or wild rice, or brown rice).

In the sizzle bizzle

Pan fry your carrots for a quick fix. Halve or quarter. Put them in a hot pan with a splash of oil. Season. Fling in some cumin or fennel seeds, or a bit of butter, honey and thyme.

Cook uncovered for a mo, then cover. Shake the pan, so they don't stick. You may need to add a bit of water. When they're tender remove the lid and cook them a little longer, to brown.

Storage tips

Carrots like the cold, so keep them in the fridge veg drawer. If they go bendy, give them a drink. Just stick them root end down in a glass of water in a cool place (the fridge) to perk them up.

VEGAN
Breakfast Cookies

These are super easy to make and brill for breakfast on the run, or to quell the 3pm snack monster.

Preheat oven to 180°C/Gas 4.

Mix the flour, oats, bicarbonate of soda and salt in a big bowl, so the bicarbonate of soda and salt are evenly distributed. Add the remaining ingredients. Mix.

Scoop it up by the tablespoon and press into rounds on an oiled baking sheet. Tidy up the edges. You'll probably get about a dozen per tray. If you don't want two batches, just freeze the rest of the mix for another day.

For chewy cookies, bake for 10 mins, or till they are just starting to set and go a little golden. For crisp cookies, flip them over and bake for another 3 mins or so.

Once cooked, they store nicely for a week in an airtight container.

- 125g wholemeal or spelt flour
- 150g jumbo porridge oats
- ½ tsp bicarbonate of soda
- ¼ tsp sea salt
- ½ tsp ground cinnamon
- 100g brown sugar
- 4 tbsp agave syrup (or honey)
- 1 large carrot, coarsely grated
- 100ml olive or coconut oil
- 100g dried fruit (raisins, blueberries, dates or apricots), chopped
- 100g nuts (almonds, hazelnuts, walnuts, brazil nuts), roughly chopped

Prep: 15 mins
Cook: 13 mins
Makes: about 24

♡ **Carrots love...**

Orange, balsamic vinegar, raisins, sunflower seeds, beef, cardamom, cinnamon, rosemary, cumin, hazelnuts, chilli, honey, ginger, lime, walnuts, lentils.

Roast Carrot Soup with Cashews & Chilli

This dairy-free soup is a big, bold, bright alternative to the classic carrot and coriander (yawn) combo.

Preheat oven to 200°C/Gas 6. Place a roasting tin in the oven to heat up.

Add the carrots, garlic and a splash of olive oil to the hot roasting tin. Season with salt and pepper. Roast till the carrots have coloured and are mashably tender, about 30 mins.

Toast your cashews till golden in a dry frying pan, or on a tray in the oven. Whizz in a food processor or pound in a pestle and mortar till it's peanut butter-like (or just use peanut butter).

Blend the carrots, nut butter and a few splashes of the stock to make a thick, smooth mash. Add chilli powder, to taste. Mix in a handful of fresh mint to counter the chilli heat.

Trickle and stir in enough stock to get the soup as thick or thin as you like. Season to taste and finish with a squeeze of lime juice.

- 8 good sized carrots, peeled and finely diced
- 2 garlic cloves, peeled and crushed
- A splash of olive oil
- Sea salt and freshly ground pepper
- 50g cashew nuts (or 2 tbsp peanut butter)
- 750ml–1 ltr warm veg stock
- A pinch of chilli powder
- A handful of fresh mint
- A squeeze of lime

Prep: 10 mins

Cook: 45 mins

Serves: 2

Seedy, Spicy Carrot Salad

Try this with beetroot (as well as, or instead of, carrots). If you have mixed salad leaves or watercress invite them to the party too.

Mix the carrots, ginger, chilli, garlic and citrus juice and zest. Drizzle in some olive oil and a pinch of salt. Toss (don't snigger, it's salad).

Let the flavours mingle for at least 15 mins, or leave in the fridge overnight.

Taste. Add a drop of agave to soften the heat, if needed. Finish with toasted seeds and coriander. Gently mix and serve.

- 4 carrots, coarsely grated
- A thumb of fresh ginger, finely grated
- 1 red chilli, deseeded and finely chopped or a pinch of chilli powder (to taste)
- 1 garlic clove, finely chopped
- 1 lemon or 2 limes, juice and zest
- A glug of olive oil
- A pinch of sea salt
- A drizzle of agave syrup (or honey)
- A large handful of sunflower and/or pumpkin seeds, toasted
- A large handful of fresh coriander, chopped

Prep: 15 mins

Cook: nil

Serves: 4

Mushrooms

Mushrooms are strange little things. The older they get, the better they taste (as long as they don't go mouldy, of course). Patrick Hearne, our organic mushroom man, digs around in the back of the fridge for the shrivelled ones as they have a more concentrated flavour.

When you cook mushrooms, fry them till they release, then re-absorb, their juices.

VEGAN

Balsamic Multipass Mushrooms

Warm a large frying pan over high heat. Sauté the mushrooms in a glug of olive oil till golden. Add the garlic and cook for a mo.

Drizzle in the balsamic vinegar. Let the mushrooms absorb it. Season to taste. Finish with fresh parsley or any other herbs you have knocking about.

Perfect with:

A poached egg on toast. Lettuce, crispy croutons and bacon. Rice with fruit and toasted seeds (instant pilaf). Pasta with chilli, rosemary and nuggets of mozzarella.

- 2–3 handfuls of mushrooms, thinly sliced
- 2 garlic cloves, peeled and finely chopped
- A glug of olive oil
- A good splash of balsamic vinegar
- Sea salt and freshly ground pepper
- A handful of fresh parsley, chopped

Prep: 5 mins
Cook: 15 mins
Serves: 2–4

How to dry mushrooms

Dry your mushrooms and they'll store for ages. It works best with white, brown or shiitake. Lay whole or sliced 'shrooms on a cloth, brown paper bag or a cake drying rack. Leave in a dry spot at room temp. They should shrivel after a few days.

When you're sure all the moisture is gone, store them in an airtight container.

Because of their richer, more intense taste, they're marvellous in veggie or beef stews, or a risotto with chives and mascarpone.

Mushroom Bolognese

Mushrooms are so meaty, you can use them instead of beef in Bolognese.

Heat a glug of oil in a large pan over medium heat. When it's hot, add the onions, garlic, carrots and celery. Sizzle till soft, 10–15 mins. Add the mushrooms. Season well. Cook till they start to pick up colour and lose some moisture.

Add the tomatoes, balsamic vinegar, wine and bay leaves. Let it bubble up and reduce. Add the tomato purée to thicken. Meanwhile, cook your pasta.

Once the pasta is done and the sauce thick, taste it. Adjust seasoning as needed. Add the herbs. Tumble the pasta through the sauce. Serve with some greenery (rocket, watercress or a handful of chopped parsley), a little drizzle of olive oil and some Parmesan.

Storage tips

Fresh mushrooms need to go in the fridge. Keep them in a cardboard tray or a paper bag. Avoid plastic or glass, as moisture makes them mouldy.

- A few glugs of olive oil
- 2 onions, finely diced
- 4 large garlic cloves, chopped
- 2 large carrots, finely diced
- 2 sticks of celery, finely diced
- 400g mushrooms (any variety), finely chopped
- Sea salt and freshly ground pepper
- 800g tinned tomatoes
- A splash of balsamic vinegar
- A glass of red wine
- 2 bay leaves (optional)
- 2 tbsp tomato purée
- A few sprigs of rosemary or thyme, leaves only
- 500g dried spaghetti
- Fresh rocket or watercress
- Freshly grated Parmesan (optional)

Prep: 20 mins

Cook: 45 mins

Serves: 4–6

Mushrooms & Toast Frittata

Heat your grill to high. Fry your mushrooms in a hot frying pan, with olive oil and/or butter, till golden. Add more oil if needed.

Add garlic and a splash of balsamic vinegar, soy sauce or a swirl of Marmite at the end.

Season. Top with herbs. Dot toast pieces around the mushrooms. Sprinkle in the cheese. Whisk and season the eggs. Pour them in the pan. Add some more herbs.

Grill till bubbly, golden and set. Grate on more cheese, if you wish. Slice into wedges. Serve.

> ♡ **Mushrooms love...**
>
> Garlic, wild garlic, spring onions, thyme, parsley, ham, balsamic vinegar, rosemary, chilli, egg, toast, blue cheese, pastry.

- 2–3 handfuls of mushrooms, sliced
- A few glugs of olive oil and/or a knob of butter
- 2 garlic cloves, finely chopped
- A glug of balsamic vinegar, soy sauce or a dollop of Marmite
- Sea salt and freshly ground pepper
- A handful of fresh herbs
- 2 slices of buttered toast, torn into bite-sized bits
- 2 big handfuls of grated cheese
- 6 eggs

Prep: 10 mins

Cook: 20 mins

Serves: 4–6

Magical Mushrooms

Our Abergavenny goat's cheese turns a punnet of mushrooms into something quite magical. Fold through cooked pasta with a splash of olive oil. Or use as a pâté or dip. Or melt it as a sauce for steak or chicken. It also freezes well.

Melt the butter and warm the oil in a frying pan. Add the mushrooms. Season well. Fry till they start to pick up colour and lose their moisture.

Add garlic and a good squeeze of lemon juice. Cook till tender. Add more oil if needed. Grate in some lemon zest. Let it cool.

Blend the cheese, herbs and cooled mushrooms till smooth. Season to taste.

- A slice of butter and a splash of olive oil
- 3 handfuls of mushrooms (any type), sliced
- Sea salt and freshly ground pepper
- 1 lemon, juice and zest
- 2 garlic cloves, finely chopped
- 100g soft, crumbly goat's cheese
- A handful of fresh tarragon or parsley leaves, roughly chopped

Prep: 15 mins

Cook: 15 mins

Serves: 2–4

Onions

Onions are pretty essential. Both of our Daves (Vegan Dave and Barefoot Running Dave) cite onions as their favourite veg. In most recipes, if you don't have an onion, a leek or shallots will do.

Golden Globes

Onions are loaded with natural sugars. You wouldn't get that impression if you chomped into one raw though, even if it is said to keep colds at bay.

If you thinly slice an onion and cook it slowly till it's super sweet and tender, you've a whole new ingredient to play with.

It doesn't matter if you cook the onions in butter or oil (but butter, because it contains its own sugars, makes them a bit sweeter). Half butter, half oil works well. Time is also key. Let the onions cook for a good 30 mins. The longer they cook, the sweeter they'll be.

Mock the weep

To avoid onion tears, keep your head as far away from the chopping onion as possible – it's the chemicals they release that make us weep, so the further you are from the rising onion gas, the better. Chilling them first, and using a sharp knife also helps.

My favourite uses for caramelised onions are...

On pizza with goat's cheese, rosemary and olives.

In quiche with snips of smoky bacon.

Mixed with quinoa or bulgar wheat with lemon juice and zest, toasted pinenuts and capers.

In a bread roll with sausages, around a bonfire with a scary ghost story.

As a side with a Sunday roast, especially with a forerib of beef.

Storage tips

Onions are fine knocking about at room temperature, and they're fine in the fridge. They're ok to eat if they start to sprout.

Onion Crackles

Amazing as a snack (think onion crisps), a garnish for a curry or a finishing touch for salads or other dishes.

Pour the oil into a pot or a deep saucepan. Place over a high heat.

In a dish, soak the onion slivers in the milk. Mix the flour, salt, pepper and spices in a bowl. Remove the onions from the milk. Thoroughly coat in the flour.

Drop a piece of coated onion into the oil. If it sizzles instantly and floats to the top, the oil's hot enough.

Fry in small batches – they'll cook faster and look better.

Fish the golden onions out with a slotted spoon. Drain on kitchen roll or in a sieve. Add a little more salt, if you like. Continue till they're all cooked.

- 1 ltr sunflower oil
- 1 large onion, halved, peeled and very thinly sliced
- ½ mug of milk
- ½ mug of plain white flour
- ½ tsp sea salt
- ½ tsp black pepper
- ½ tsp paprika
- A pinch of chilli powder (optional)

Prep: 10 mins

Cook: 15 mins

Serves: 4

Undercover Onion Tart

This French onion tart will clear your onion backlog. It tastes so delicious it might just bring a tear to your eye. It'll be that, or the realisation you're not in France. (It's so good though, that you won't mind.) Serve with seasonal salad and a nice glass of chilled rosé.

Sift the flour with a good pinch of salt into a large bowl. Cut 70g of the butter into small cubes and add to the bowl. Coat them in flour then rub the flour into the butter with cold fingers (the secret to great pastry) till it resembles breadcrumbs.

Add the beaten egg and just enough cold water (2–3 tbsp) to make a soft dough. Place in a small bowl, cover and chill for 30 mins.

Preheat the oven to 180°C/Gas 4.

In a heavy-bottomed pan, melt the remaining butter. Add the onions and sugar; cook for 30 mins over a medium–low heat, stirring often. Season. Stir in the thyme. Set aside.

Roll the dough on a floured surface till thin. Carefully place in a lightly buttered, 20 cm tart tin (ideally with a removable base). Line with greaseproof paper, add baking beans, dried beans or coins. Bake for 20 mins. When it's done, remove the paper and beans/coins.

Mix the egg yolks, créme fraîche, salt and pepper. Drain any fat off the onions. Spoon them into the pastry. Spread the egg mix over the top. Turn the oven up to 190°C/Gas 5 and bake for 30–35 mins, till golden on top. Serve warm, cold or at room temperature.

- 170g plain white flour
- Sea salt and freshly ground pepper
- 120g unsalted butter, chilled
- 1 whole egg, beaten, plus 3 yolks
- 2–3 tbsp cold water
- 4 large onions (red or white), sliced very thinly
- 2 tsp caster sugar
- 2 sprigs of fresh thyme, leaves only (dried thyme will work too)
- 200g crème fraîche (half-fat is fine)

Prep: 30 mins
Cook: 1 hr
Serves: 4–6

♡ **Onions love...**

Pork, rosemary, sage, thyme, tomatoes, cumin, turmeric, mushrooms, black pudding, cloves, garlic, liver, potatoes.

Potatoes

If it wasn't for potatoes, you wouldn't be reading this now. I started Abel & Cole in 1988 with a dream and a sack of spuds. They're still my favourite food. From nutty, waxy new spuds in April to big fluffy bakers in October, they're just so fantastically versatile.

Smashing tips

For the best mashed potatoes ever, bake your spuds first, like you're making a jacket potato.

Once done, leave to cool a bit then scoop out the flesh. Mash with butter or use olive oil, like the Spanish do.

For a treat, roast the leftover skins with grated cheddar and/or bits of cooked bacon till crisp and golden.

Ain't no sunshine

Unlike most of us, potatoes don't like sunshine. They go green and sprouty. So keep them in a dark, dry, fairly cool place.

If they develop green spots or sprouting bits just trim them. If they really start to sprout, plant them! One potato can produce as much as 1–2kg of new spuds.

Super Spud Rösti

Röstis are a quick and easy way to shift a stack of spuds. If you want to experiment, add grated roots (parsnip, celeriac, etc) to the mix.

Mix the potato, onion and garlic in a bowl. Season well. Add herbs or spices, if using. Mix in the fat and flour.

Heat a frying pan over medium-heat. Add a 1 cm layer of oil or fat to the pan.

Shape the mix into balls – somewhere between a golf and a tennis ball. Squeeze out any liquid. Press into the pan, creating a rounded thin cake, sort of Scotch pancake sized. (You can make one big, thin cake, but it's easier to flip smaller röstis.)

Slowly does it. The spuds need to cook all the way through. Crank up the heat at the end to crisp up, pressing the röstis into the pan with a spatula.

Serve for brunch with grilled bacon, tomato and egg. Or alongside roast meat, or simply with a salad.

- 1 big or 2 medium potatoes, scrubbed and grated
- 1 small or ½ a large onion, finely chopped
- 1 garlic clove, finely chopped
- Sea salt and freshly ground pepper
- A handful of herbs (finely chopped sage is ace) or a pinch of spice (try caraway)
- 1 tbsp olive oil, goose fat or beef dripping
- More oil/fat for cooking
- 2 tbsp plain white flour

Prep: 10 mins

Cook: 20 mins

Makes: 4–6

Perfect Roasties

Crisp and golden on the outside. Light and fluffy as a cloud on the inside. That's a good roastie.

And for that you need the right kind of potato – a floury one.

The best in the whole entire world is arran victory but they're only really around at Christmas. So next best are maris piper, desiree and King Edwards.

The next trick is in the cooking. Follow these tips and you could win Masterchef.

Peel your spuds. Halve or quarter – leave them quite chunky.

Boil in salted water till they're soft, but not totally falling apart.

Drain. Cool. Refrigerate uncovered. This dries them out a bit, which helps crisp the skin.

Preheat your oven to 200°C/Gas 6.

Give the spuds a little shake in a sieve or dish to duff up the sides. These bits will go crispy. Duff, duff, duff. Season.

Warm some goose fat, beef dripping, rapeseed or sunflower oil in a roasting tray till smoking hot.

Gently spoon the cold spuds through the hot fat so they're nicely coated.

Roast till golden, 45 mins–1 hr. Check them often. Add a scattering of fresh rosemary and grated lemon zest right towards the end.

Season with sea salt and serve.

♡ **Potatoes love...**

Egg, sausages, olives, anchovies, chorizo, capers, mayo, sausages, lemon, mint, pork, smoked fish, watercress, celery, fennel, cumin, sausages.

To POTATOES, and BEYOND!

> The chipping forecast is looking good. Think beyond potatoes. Expand your chipping horizons. Loads of veg can be chipped.

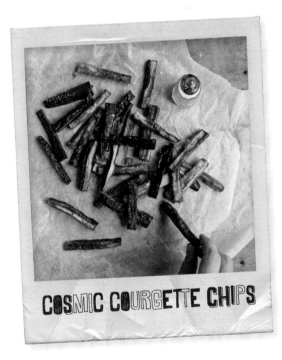

COSMIC COURGETTE CHIPS

ROOT AND TUBER CHIPS

Our favourite veg in this category include:

- Swede
- Celeriac
- Sweet potato
- Parsnips
- Normal spuds, of course – Pink Fir Apple potatoes make remarkably good chips

To turn them into chips, peel (definitely peel swede and celeriac, the rest are fine with a scrub), cut into fingers or wedges.

Shallow fry in a film of oil till crisp and golden. Or heat a large baking tray in a warming oven (200°C/Gas 6). In a bowl, lightly coat the raw chips in oil and sea salt. Put them on the hot tray and roast till crisp, gold and tender.

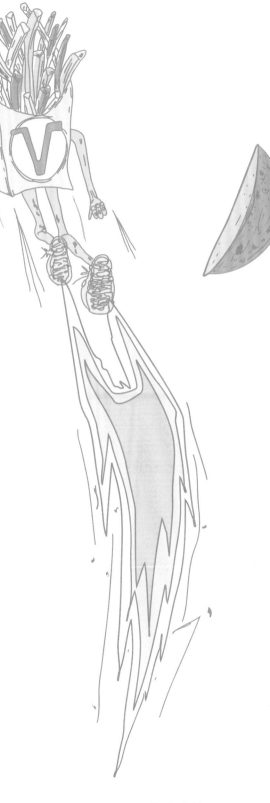

A CHIP FOR ALL SEASONINGS

Classic chips

A pinch of sea salt, a squeeze of lemon juice and some freshly ground black pepper will bring a little buzz to your chips.

Italian chips

Dust your chips with Parmesan and chilli powder – let the chips cool a tick before grating the cheese over them.

Rocket chips

Right at the end of cooking, dust some spices over your chips. Use a pack of Masala spice or make your own. Ground cumin, turmeric, mustard seeds, ginger and chilli are out of this world.

About thyme chips

Sprinkle some finely chopped rosemary or thyme leaves over the chips towards the end of cooking, along with a bit of finely grated lemon zest.

Green chips

Transform the humble courgette into cosmic chips. Chop your courgette into batons and dust them in seasoned flour. Pan fry them in hot oil till lush and golden on all sides.

Spanish Potatoes

Boil your spuds in salted water till just tender. Drain and cool a little.

Warm a large frying pan. Gloss with oil. Add the onion, spuds, salt and pepper. Cook on medium heat till the onion softens and the spuds start to pick up colour.

Stir in the red pepper and add the spices till the pepper softens.

Add the citrus juice and zest and the vinegar. Cook a touch longer. Taste. Adjust seasoning.

Sprinkle fresh herbs over the top if you have any.

Omnivorous options: Slice up some chorizo and add with the pepper, or top it with a poached or fried egg.

- 4 good-sized potatoes, peeled and cubed
- A good splash of olive oil
- 1 onion, thinly sliced
- 1 red pepper, deseeded and cubed (optional)
- 1 tsp ground cumin
- 1 tsp paprika
- A good pinch of chilli powder
- 1 orange, a lemon or 2 limes, juice and zest
- A splash of vinegar
- Sea salt and freshly ground pepper
- A handful of fresh herbs

Prep: 10 mins

Cook: 30–45 mins

Serves: 2–4

VEGETARIAN
Rustic Irish Potato Bread

Stunning with butter and marmalade, or a weekend fry up.

Boil your spuds in salted water till mashable. Drain. Mash (or use a potato ricer) with a good knob of butter and a pinch of salt.

Sift the flour, little by little, into the mash till it forms a soft dough. The exact amount will depend on the moisture content of the potatoes, so use your judgement. Keep adding flour till the dough is soft and no longer sticky.

Roll it out on a floured surface so it's about 1 cm thick. Dust with extra flour as you roll and cut. Tidy the edges and cut into squares. It'll look rustic but that's what you're after.

Place in a large frying pan over high heat – no need for oil or butter. Turn the heat down after a few mins. Cook on each side till golden. Dab a bit of butter on the bread once cooked.

- 500g potatoes, peeled and cubed
- A knob of butter
- 1–2 mugs of plain white flour
- A good pinch of sea salt

Prep: 15 mins

Cook: 20 mins

Serves: 4

Red pepper

If you've been to the flicks recently you may have heard the dulcet tones of Redd Pepper; a London tube driver turned Hollywood voiceover artist. I really hope he did the voiceover for the Ratatouille trailer.

Pep talk
. . . .

Sweet heavens

Roasting red peppers intensifies their sweetness as the natural sugars caramelise. Just pop 'em whole into a 200°C/Gas 6 oven and cook till blackened and collapsingly tender. Turn once or twice.

Red most roast

Plonk a whole roasted pepper on a plate with steak, chips and salad. Or, peel the skin (when cool) and tear into ribbons, discarding the seeds. Ace in salad, or sandwiched with crumbled feta and basil.

Roll the dice

Raw diced pepper is perfect in an Asian salsa with mini cubes of pineapple, desiccated coconut, soy sauce, ginger, fresh chilli, lime and coriander. Lovely with fish.

Storage tips

They may grow in hot climes but once they're picked, your peppers like to chill out in the fridge.

♡ Red pepper loves...

Other Mediterranean veg (olives, aubergine, courgette, onion, tomatoes, garlic), houmous, shellfish, noodles, potatoes, chilli, basil, ginger, feta.

Sauce It Up, Romesco Style

This is our version of a seductive, smoky Spanish sauce from Catalonia. Great with pasta, as a dip, for bruschetta, a stuffing for chicken... whatever you fancy really.

Heat your oven to 200°C/Gas 6.

Roast your peppers for about 20 mins. They're done when they're all soft and the skin is charred (not to be confused with chard, because that's green).

Toast the almonds in a warm frying pan. Then remove the nuts and fry the bread in a splash of oil till golden. Whizz up the nuts and bread with the garlic, paprika and chilli and a little oil till it forms a paste. You may need to do it in batches.

Let the peppers cool a bit. Strip off the skin. Deseed. Add the flesh and a splash of oil and the vinegar to the almond mix. Blend till fairly smooth. Season. Add more oil if needed.

Loosen a little with lemon juice, water and olive oil if serving with pasta.

Keeps in the fridge for 3–4 days and freezes well.

- 1 large or 2 smaller red peppers
- A good handful of almonds
- 1 large slice of stale bread, torn into pieces
- A few glugs of olive oil
- 2 garlic cloves, peeled
- ½ tsp sweet paprika
- A pinch of chilli powder
- Sea salt and freshly ground pepper
- 1 tbsp red wine or cider vinegar
- A little lemon juice

Prep: 20 mins

Cook: 35 mins

Serves: 4

Bananas

The banana plant is not a tree, but the largest flowering herb in the world. They are the most popular fruit in Britain, but sadly one of the most wasted. If only everyone knew how versatile they are, and that they freeze so well...

Quick fixes

The richest, creamiest milkshake in the world

Frozen bananas make ace smoothies and milkshakes. No need for ice cream, either. For two milkshakes, whizz three frozen bananas in a blender or food processor with 300–400ml milk (dairy, soya or nut). For a flourish add vanilla, cocoa powder or berries.

Instant ice cream

Frozen bananas make instant, sugar-free ice cream. Simply blitz frozen banana pieces with a drop of crème fraîche or coconut milk. Pretend your food processor is an ice cream machine; churn and pulsate till it's thick, cold and creamy.

Experiment with flavours. Try adding cocoa powder, peanut butter, cardamom, a splash of cold coffee, toasted walnuts, lime juice, nutmeg, tahini or vanilla. (Maybe not all at once.)

Cat's green banana curry

Cat is our most green minded gal. If your bananas aren't ripening, peel and slice into thickish chunks. Chuck them in a coconuty Thai-style curry towards the end of the cooking time.

Transformer chutney

This works with bananas that are not too ripe, and not too green. It's tops with curry.

Peel and dice two bananas. Mix with a pinch of sea salt, a splash of cider vinegar, black pepper, ground cloves, a hint of cinnamon, finely chopped fresh chilli, a little grated ginger and a pinch of sugar. Mix thoroughly. Taste and add one or more of the above ingredients as needed, till it's sweet and tangy.

Storage tips

If your bananas are green, pop them in a paper bag with a tomato or a kiwi to ripen them.

If you have a glut of over ripe bananas, make banana loaf (or freeze, P.T.O.).

Paul's Steamed Banana Puds with Cardamom Toffee

Heat your oven to 180°C/Gas 4.

Rub the inside of 6 ramekins or ovenproof tea cups (about 150ml capacity) with butter. Dust with flour, then shake out any excess.

Whip butter and sugar till pale and creamy. Use a hand mixer, food processor, or a good old fashioned whisk.

Whisk the eggs into the butter and sugar mix till it's light and fluffy. (If you're using your arms, know that it's worth it.)

Beat in the mashed bananas and coconut or dates. Sift in the flour and salt.

Gently mix. Divide between ramekins or cups. The mix should come about half way up. Wrap each vessel in foil. Place in a roasting tray and pour in enough boiling water to come half way up the vessels.

Bake till set, about 30 mins.

Meanwhile, make the toffee sauce. Put all the ingredients in a saucepan over a low heat. Stir till the sugar dissolves and the sauce thickens and darkens.

Drizzle the sauce over the warm puddings and stop drooling, just tuck in.

- 100g butter, softened
- 100g caster sugar
- 2 eggs
- 2 ripe bananas, mashed to a paste
- 50g desiccated coconut or finely chopped dates
- 100g self-raising flour (or 100g plain white flour + 1½ tsp baking powder), plus extra for dusting
- A pinch of sea salt

For the toffee sauce:
- 100g unsalted butter
- 100g light muscovado sugar
- 125ml double cream
- Crushed seeds from 3 cardamom pods

Prep: 20 mins
Cook: 30 mins
Makes: 6

Life in the freezer

Bananas freeze beautifully. If bananas go brown, you're sitting on a gold mine. Just peel and pop them in a container and shove them in the freezer. Keep in freezy hibernation till the urge to bake grabs you.

Kiwi

Sometimes, at certain times of the year, a small, fuzzy kiwi mountain can grow in the fruit bowl. Kiwis are packed with vitamin C and our Super Ted Bell eats them whole, skin and all. That's one way to get your fibre (even if it is a little bit like eating a doormat).

Kwik fixes

Kiwinder egg

My favourite way to eat a kiwi is to pretend it's a boiled egg. Use an egg cup, then slice and scoop. For a bit of fun (and a treat), serve with cinnamon and sugar dusted toast soldiers.

The whole fruit

As the skin is perfectly edible you can bite into it like an apple or slice it into beautiful discs.

Kwake

Kiwi is tops in cake. Peel and slice into rounds. Brush a baking dish with butter. Dust with caster sugar. Cover the bottom of the tin with your kiwi slices. Pour in a classic sponge mixture. Swirl some finely chopped white chocolate into the cake batter first, if you like. Bake. Invert and you've got a white chocolate kiwi upside down cake.

Kwocktails

Diced kiwi makes pretty 'ice cubes'. Freeze and have in a G&T. Or whizz frozen fruit to a purée, strain and make cocktails (think mojito!).

Health kwick

For a vitamin packed smoothie, whizz up peeled and diced kiwi and banana with apple juice and vanilla yogurt.

♡ **Kiwi loves...**

Apple, orange, banana, cinnamon, vanilla ice cream, white chocolate, cake, Pimms, lime.

Mango

Nocturnal, shy, looks good in a pinny; the hedgehog is a curious creature. Ours is less spiky and more fruity than your common or garden Mrs Tiggywinkle.

How to make an orange hedgehog

Give your mango a squeeze. If there's a bit of give it's ripe and ready to hedgehog.

Stand the mango on its end. Carve off the two fleshy cheeks either side of the flat stone in the middle.

Slice a criss cross pattern into the inside of each half, without cutting through the skin.

Invert by pushing in the middle of the skin side. Slice or bite off the bits.

Use in salads, smoothies or get stuck in straight away. Eat any flesh around the remaining middle stone bit too.

Pineapple

The UK fruit season is a few months short of a year, so in those months we thank the fantastic fairtrade farmers in far-ish flung climes for their tropical fruit.

Pining for a dining

If the dice is rice

Pineapple is gorgeous in fried rice. Roughly dice along with veg, like red peppers and courgettes. Thinly slice spring onions or a leek. Sizzle everything together with ginger, chilli and garlic. Splash in some soy sauce. Stir through cooked rice. Add some egg, leftover roast chicken or pork, or toasted cashews.

Mr Freeze & Mr Whippy

Pineapple freezes beautifully. Dice what you don't eat fresh. Freeze it and use it from frozen (in the above recipe for example). Or whizz in a food processor with vanilla seeds or essence till it blends into an incredible sugar-free sorbet.

80's revival

It's retrotastic, but pineapple is radical on a stick with cheese (great for children's lunchboxes) or in ham and cheese toasties.

Storage tips

This large dude is chilled enough as it is. It's fine at room temp and will ripen a little more (if needed). To tell if it's ripe, sniff the base. If it's fragrant, it's ready to eat.

♡ Pineapple loves...

Vanilla, ginger, chilli, cinnamon, ice cream, pork, crispy-skinned fish, red pepper, cucumber, spring onions, mint, basil.

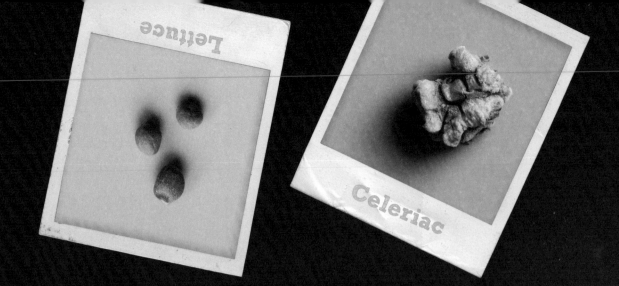
Lettuce

Celeriac

From small weird shapes grow lunch

If you've ever grown your own, you'll know how life affirming it is to plant a teeny little seed, watch it sprout and (hopefully) grow into something you can harvest and have for supper.

Parsnip

Chicory

Beetroot

Cabbage

Pineapple

Radish

Cucumber

Carrot

We've jumbled these up

Can you guess what grows into what? (Answers on page 249.)

Fridges and freezers and what goes where

To blanch

Not a letter to a Tennessee Williams character, but the most useful method for freezing veg. Plunge your veg into boiling water for a minute or two, then douse with cold water if freezing.

Brassicas

Brassicas should go in the fridge.

If you don't have space, cabbage is ok at cool room temp. You may just need to peel off the outer leaves before cooking.

The best way to preserve green and white cabbage is to sauerkraut or pickle.

Red cabbage freezes very well after braising.

Blanch broccoli and cauli for a few secs before freezing. Defrost fully before cooking.

Potatoes and roots

Potatoes need a cold dark place. So do roots (the fridge, in most cases).

Cooked spuds and roots freeze very well, especially if mashed or roasted first.

Lettuces and leaves

Keep these guys in the fridge, and out of plastic.

They really don't like freezers (unless they've been cooked into a quiche or something similar).

Spinach is the only exception. Wilt it down, squeeze out excess water and freeze in an ice cube tray. When defrosted, it's perfect for pizza toppings or quiche.

Tomatoes

Keep tomatoes in the fridge, especially in warm weather. But warm to room temperature before eating them. They'll taste much better – especially if they sit on a sunny windowsill for a bit.

Tomatoes are great to freeze. Just pop them in a lidded tub. Ex-frozen tomatoes are especially good in stews and sauces.

Aubergine, courgettes and red peppers

Keep all of these in the fridge.

To freeze aubergines turn them into a dip like baba ganoush first. (Shameless plug: a recipe for which you'll find in my first book.)

Raw courgettes freeze well if grated first. Perfect in the cakes on page 168.

Peppers freeze best when roasted whole till tender and blackened. Tear them into ribbons, scrape out the seeds and remove the loose skin. Freeze and use on pizza or in a pasta sauce.

Asparagus and Summer beans

Keep asparagus and beans in the fridge.

Roast, steam or blanch asparagus before freezing.

Blanch beans for a few mins before freezing.

Apples and pears

These kids are happy in a fruit bowl and in the fridge. To freeze, dice or slice and toss with lemon juice, or compote first.

Stone fruit

Wait till they (peach, plums, nectarines, apricots, cherries) ripen, then refrigerate.

To freeze, cut into segments and toss in lemon juice (to stop them discolouring). Once defrosted, use in crumbles, pies or compote.

Frozen mango tastes like sorbet. Cut into strips, freeze and eat on a hot day.

Berries, currants and rhubarb too

Keep these in the fridge. They freeze beautifully. Put raw whole fruits (chop rhubarb) on a tray with space between them. Freeze. Then tip into a container or freezer bag and put them back in the freezer. Perfect for baking, jamming or compoting on a rainy day.

Bananas

Keep these guys away from the fridge. However, if they're ripe, they're perfect for freezing. Peel and freeze whole, or cut into pieces.

Keep it in the family

You can choose your friends...
and you can choose your vegetables.

Allium family
Alliaceae

Chives
Garlic
Leeks
Onions
Shallots

Brassica or mustard family
Cruciferae

Broccoli
Brussels sprouts
Cabbage
Cauliflower
Chinese leaf
Horseradish
Kale
Kohlrabi
Mustard
Radish
Turnip
Wasabi
Watercress

Carrot family
Apiaceae

Caraway
Carrots
Celeriac
Celery
Coriander
Cumin
Dill
Fennel
Parsley
Parsnips

Daisy family
Asteraceae

Chamomile
Chicory
Dandelion
Globe artichoke
Jerusalem artichokes
Lettuce
Salsify (Scorzonera)
Sunflower
Tarragon

Goosefoot family
Chenopodiaceae

Beetroot
Chard
Quinoa
Spinach

Good Gourd family*
Cucurbitaceae

Courgettes
Cucumber
Marrow
Melon
Pumpkin
Squash

*Abel & Coleism

Fennel

Salsify

Grasses family
Poaceae

Barley
Corn
Oats
Rice
Rye
Wheat

Legume family
Fabaceae

Alfalfa
Bean
Clover
Lentils
Pea
Peanut
Soybean

Nightshade family
Solanaceae

Aubergine
Chilli
Pepper
Potato
Tomatoes

Any keen horticulturist will note that this list of plant families is not exhaustive, but it covers the popular kids.

Celeriac

Kohlrabi

Never eat a raw potato and other wisdom bites...

Never eat a raw potato

Potatoes are my favourite vegetable but they are part of the nightshade family (you may know their distant cousin, Deadly...). The leaves and stems of the plant are poisonous. But as long as you cut off any green or sprouting bits, and you cook them, they're as benign as a puppy on a cushion.

Don't stalk a tomato

Tomatoes, like their relatives the potato, have leaves and stalks that are best avoided. As an aside, the fruit of a potato plant looks just like a tomato. Don't get them confused though, as you'll get a mouthful of seeds and a tummy ache.

Sometimes cook tomatoes

It has been reported in the Journal of Agriculture and Food Chemistry, that even though tomatoes may lose some vitamin C when cooked, cooking them substantially raises the levels of beneficial compounds called phytochemicals.

Cooking enhances lycopene content in tomatoes. Lycopene is a phytochemical that gives tomatoes their red colour and is a known antioxidant.

Eat more nettles

You only need some thick gardening gloves to forage the main ingredient for soups, stews, beer and a nice cup of tea.

'Brotchan Neanntog' (try saying that after a couple of homebrew nettle beers) is a traditional Irish broth made from nettles. Our bright Swede Sara, makes delicious nettle pesto.

The sting of a nettle is in their little silicone hairs. Once crushed, they won't sting. Soaking them in water or cooking also removes the sting. Forage forever with tips from www.selfsufficientish.com

Eat less meat

We know that eating more plants than meat is healthy, and lots of people are naturally following a semi-vegetarian diet.

A study cited in New Scientist by Jim Giles, added up the costs of modern day meat-heavy diets. It concluded that cutting back on beefburgers and bacon could wipe $20 trillion - hang about, twenty trillion dollars - off the cost of fighting climate change.

Throw away your phone and grow your own

Creating a little distance between the human and the handheld device (phone, iPad, GameBoy) is a Very Good Thing to do. If you've not quite mastered the art of meditating to a higher state of consciousness, find a little peace in gardening.

Even without a garden you can garden. Windowsill veg plots will at least give you herbs and the odd edible nasturtium. Get a helping hand at www.gardenorganic.org.uk

Cook from scratch

Cooking is like gardening. Therapeutic. Chopping veg, measuring out spices, slicing a lemon in half... Your mind has time to wander, which is crucial for problem solving and creative decision making. If you've exhausted this book, find even more recipes at www.abelandcole.co.uk/recipes

Acknowledgements

This Veg Box Companion made many friends in the three months (a wildly short time) it went from a twinkle in my eye, to a fully reared cookbook. So some very big thank yous are due.

To the Abel & Cole-ers who contributed recipes. To Paul Freestone for pages 49, 188 and 230, Hella Jozsa for page 21, Nick Briggs for page 132, Emma Stringer for page 64, Gary Congress for page 92, Fiona Chalmers for the idea (and for being a fantastic tester) on 190, Trudy Bridgeman-Rivett, Ruth Brown, Casie Draper for their tips on page 34, and Catriona Coull for the tip on page 228. And the gloriously talented Rachel de Thample for everything else.

Many thanks to The Tartlettes for their hot dates on page 102. And thank you to Hector Browne for his excellent stick retrieval.

To the massively fabulous team of Abel & Cole testers, proofers and tweakers (most of whom volunteered time to help): Emma Healey, Kalvyn fFrench-James, Clare Mansfield, Alison Triggs, Anne Parkes, Safia Haleem, Tamara Jevons, Catherine Booysen, Katy Finnis, Nicky Browning, Joanne Williams, Sarah Williams, Lucy Stepan, Fred Mackenzie, Cathy Laurence, Claire Amzaleg, Tabatha Coe, Clare Bland, Emily Smith, Fern Albert, Jon Chappell, Joss Walford, Rhiannon Larkman, Lucy Button, Gabby Bignell, Sinéad Lawlor, Dan Chilcott, Marta Salva, Simon Rees and Lauren Ward. And to Heather Gorringe of Wiggly Wigglers for her sound advice on composting.

A special thank you to Sara Haglund and Nicky Browning for being absolute super stars. And to Michael Dane, man with the the tightest jeans in the office.

To my fellow team cookbookers, Rachel de Thample, Claudia Ruane, Graham Cousins and Gary Congress, for being such brilliantly bookish types, thank you.

This book is dedicated to my family Chippy, Jessica and Hugo, and to all the farmers, makers and bakers who give us something to cook.

And to every single Abel & Cole customer, past and present (and Suzie), for giving us a reason to write recipes, box up veg and find out where the word for avocado comes from.

Thank you.

Illustrations
Michael Dane: 36, 37, 82, 83, 90, 91, 122, 123, 174, 175, 186, 187, 190, 191, 224, 225, 235.
Graham Cousins: 26, 27, 42, 43, 52, 53, 88, 89, 126, 127, 138, 139, 146, 147.